GAME

PHIL VICKERY & SIMON BODDY

GAME

NEW WAYS TO PREPARE, COOK & CURE

PHOTOGRAPHY BY PETER CASSIDY

KYLE BOOKS

Contents

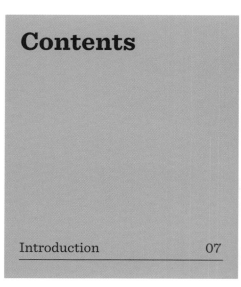

3
Wildfowl

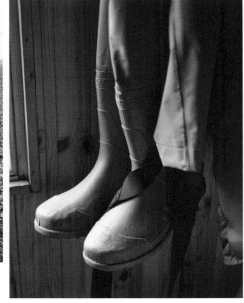

4
Fish

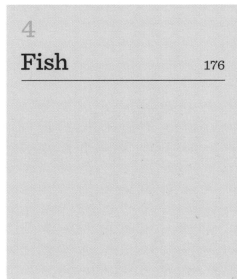

5
Basics

Introduction

My two brothers and I grew up in a small terraced house in the seaside town of Folkestone, Kent. It had a tiny garden that backed onto the main railway line to London. The trains ran all night and were quite noisy but you got used to it. Playing in the street was what you did, and a trip to the park was considered a 'day out'. Occasionally, my dad took me to the local canal where we would fish for tiny roach or perch. Now that was a real day out! I remember being so excited I could hardly sleep the night before and would spend hours getting ready and checking all the gear. I say all the gear; it was an old Oxo tin filled with a few floats, bits of old line and lead weights. I still treasure them to this day. I can remember asking my dad why we never took the fish home to eat. He would say they were too small, but that when we caught a whopper we would. He must have known that was never going to happen.

As my brothers and I got older, Dad would take us cockling with an old rake. We would spend hours at low tide on the beach near New Romney raking through sand banks and getting a fair haul. Shrimping was also good fun. This involved wading through small pools and along the shoreline with makeshift nets made from broom handles and Mum's old net curtains. It certainly worked; we would have a pretty good feed when we got home. Dad also made a crab net from a discarded bicycle wheel, spokes removed, a net curtain again sewn around the rim with string. An old fish head was attached to the two pieces of string, that lay across the centre. The wheel was secured with a long piece of thin rope and hurled off Folkestone Pier. We would wait with excitement for a few minutes and then haul it in to see if we had caught anything. More often than not we did quite well and I can still remember seeing a cooked whole crab in my brother's Pinky & Perky (two puppet pig characters from the 1960s) bowl in the fridge.

One day, my mum and dad decided they wanted to move to the 'country'. Yes, the country. This, I now realise, meant only a few miles into the hills but, at the age of eight, it felt like going into another world entirely. They looked at quite a few houses, including one by an old disused railway line, which is the only one I distinctly recall. They finally settled on a small, two-bedroomed detached house next to a farm. I can remember seeing it for the first time. It was amazing, as it had a huge garden in which we could ride our bikes, plus a garden shed or den. Not only that, the farm had barns full of hay and straw – another playground. The field opposite had trees for us to climb and suspend rope swings from, and five minutes' walk across the fields there was a huge wood.

We were encouraged to get out of the house and explore the fields and ponds. It was so exciting. The farmer, a Mr Munn, would let us watch the milking of the cows and the feeding of the calves. And when my teacher found out where we had moved to, we even had a school trip to see how a farm was run. Over the next couple of years, I learnt so much about wildlife – about birds' nests, duck nests, bats, rats, newts and frogs – just from watching for hours on end.

But it was the wood where we spent all our holidays, building camps and tree houses, only coming back home for food. No mobile phones, no contact, just great fun getting muddy and a having a good time. Occasionally, my dad would come with us and rig up long ropes across a small dell. We would then sit in a rope loop with a pulley on top and glide

> "Seasonality of cooking has also always excited me. The first grouse in late summer, the first wild duck and partridge in early autumn and pheasant a few weeks later are events I look forward to. Knowing that you only have a limited time to enjoy Nature's bounty makes cooking a pleasurable experience."

down. It was heaven. For the most part, though, our parents were glad to get rid of us.

As I got older, my good friend Mark Howard would come over to play. I was really jealous since he had a ferret and I couldn't have one because Dad said they stank. Together, Mark and I would go to the woods, net the holes, put the ferret down and wait. It was exiting, as you could hear the rabbits thumping underground, waiting to bolt. Out they would fly straight into the nets and we would quite regularly get two or three. Problems occurred only when the ferret caught a rabbit. She would eat it and then go to sleep, which meant you had to do dig it out. This could take hours! So it was always a great relief when she appeared after the rabbit had been dispatched.

In my teens, as I described in my book *Pork*, I worked part time on Mr Munn's farm. With the farmer's son I shot the occasional rabbit and pigeon and even bagged my first hen pheasant. I took it home and hung it in my dad's greenhouse. He plucked it and Mum roasted it. This was before I had decided to study cooking.

On Friday nights at that time there was a great TV programme called *Out Of Town*, presented by the late Jack Hargreaves. The show was filmed in an old shed, probably made to look like his own. Jack Hargreaves would just chat (apparently unscripted) about his week in the country and I found it fascinating. He covered all country subjects, ranging from pigeon shooting, fly fishing and making a wooden wheel for an old cart to Morris dancing. All of it great advice that I still use today. For instance, he would crush cooked cockle and oyster shells with a garden roller and leave the chickens to pick them up as 'It made their eggs shells firmer'. My brother Mike recently bought me a box collection of *Out Of Town*, now on DVD, for Christmas. I love them. I think this was when I really became hooked on the country way of life.

Over the subsequent years I have continued to appreciate the wild food that is around us. As a chef, I have always got immense pleasure from cooking all that the countryside can provide. Local fruit, vegetables, herbs, nuts, fish and, of course, game have always featured heavily in the restaurants I have cooked in over the past 30 years. Seasonality of cooking has also always excited me. The first grouse in late summer, the first wild duck and partridge in early autumn and pheasant a few weeks later are events I look forward to. Knowing that you only have a limited time to enjoy Nature's bounty makes cooking a more enjoyable experience. Now, of course, it's cool and hip to be cooking 'wild food'. I applaud that, and long may it continue. Having said that, a lot of game cookery is still a bit old fashioned. Some dishes will survive and do well. Raised game pie, salmis of duck or pheasant and rabbit pie are all delicious. Some I hope I will never have to prepare, cook or eat again. Pheasant hung 'until green and maggot infested' (for an old client) and stinking jugged hare are a couple of examples of the sort of cooking that should never have happened in the first place. So with all this in mind, I have decided to be quite controversial and give a selection of recipes that hopefully will inspire you to seek out, prepare and cook game in all sorts of ways.

Game is a particularly good source of protein. Take, for example, venison. Mostly, it's wild or reared on a naturally balanced diet with no hormones, additives or growth promoters, so is extremely low in fat. In fact, it's so low in fat you might occasionally have to add some! It's also hugely versatile and can be made into any dish where minced meat is required. Not only that, there are very strict seasons for game. This means it is sustainable and is only eaten when in prime condition; this applies to birds, furred game, cloven hoofed game and fish. Surely that's the hard sell over!

You always know food fashions are changing when the supermarkets start to stock something. Ten years ago, you may have found a bit of game in store. Now supermarkets are full of game mix packs, wild duck, partridge, rabbit and pheasants in season. Last year, a couple of the discounters were selling a frozen, part-boned, stuffed pheasant for two people. It was cooked from frozen and, I kid you not, it was excellent. This is all good news and hopefully sales will continue to grow. Finally, yes finally, home cooks are looking beyond dry crumbly roast pheasant and good old Bambi and embracing this fabulous food.

One of the reasons I decided to write this book was to really take a new and modern approach to game cookery. Gone is the same old stuff, the mostly passed down or regurgitated waffle, and in are some new observations. Let's start with pheasant and red-legged partridge. I have never in 30 years of cooking cooked these two successfully and consistently. Even if you pick a young hen pheasant, it's still hit and miss. Likewise, with red-legged partridge, roasting it is always disappointing and you end up with dry, tasteless, tough meat. Even wrapping it in bacon doesn't work and, in my eyes, is a waste of time. Nowadays, there are 40-odd species of pheasant on offer, but you must remember they are bred for flying, not eating. Flick through the game magazines in late spring and you'll see adverts for poults (baby birds) accompanied by words such as 'great fliers'. Forget flying, the chef will love them. Red-legged partridge are the same. Grey partridge, on the other hand, which are seldom seen for sale, are poles apart. Delicious, tasty game meat with good flavour, they make a perfect meal. You will not see a recipe for roast whole pheasant or partridge in this book. What I do give is instructions for removing the breast meat, wrapping it in very thinly sliced air-dried ham and cooking it gently in butter or oil for a few minutes on both sides. That's my recipe for getting the best out of today's modern birds. Juicy, tasty and slightly undercooked is the only way.

Hares and rabbits are great when young and in season. Hare fillets sautéed and pink in salads or broths are a delight. Young wild rabbits fried, in a pie, or again in a salad are delicious. Woodcock, snipe and grouse are equally tasty and can be cooked with very good results. These can be roasted successfully and without the need for bacon. They can also be braised, sautéed and made into exquisite pâtés and terrines. Wild duck and geese need careful cooking but are delicious too. Pink roasted duck breast, braised goose in red wine are a couple of examples of how good they can be. Sea and river fish also feature in the book and I class them as game. They include: pike, carp, trout, salmon, char, crayfish, zander and eels. Some lovely modern dishes that go far beyond jellied eels (which I adore, incidentally).

A couple of years ago, I was very lucky to film and stay on three game reserves in Namibia. The wild animals were truly spectacular and it was a privilege to see them. The head chef of one honoured me by cooking some 12 species from blue wildebeest to gemsbok and kudu. All were not only delicious but also extremely good for you. He explained that to keep the herds healthy and thriving they must cull the meat, so why not eat it? I have adapted some recipes to feature some of these delicious meats.

I really hope that this book goes some way to encourage you to cook more wild meat and fish. Provided it's controlled and regulated, as it largely is, we can enjoy it with a clear conscience.

1 FEATHERED

Feathered

How long you should hang feathered game is a much debated subject – one that can cause many a heated argument, but it can really make or break a delicious meal. Firstly, it depends on the bird that you have shot and by that I mean the age and possibly the sex. A young hen pheasant bird, for example, will obviously cook differently to a wily old cock pheasant. Secondly, it depends on the time of year. A lovely young partridge shot on a warm late summer, early autumn day will only need a day or so at room temperature. In winter, however, when the temperature outside can be colder than in a fridge, it can take a week or so. Thirdly, it really depends on how strong you want the flavour to be. I, personally, have never enjoyed cooking or eating stinking, green, putrid flesh. As general rule of thumb, therefore, one to two days in late summer and early autumn is sufficient for all birds. Come late autumn and winter, I would hang birds for four to five days, sometimes a week if the weather is particularly cold. The only bird I eat fresh, with no hanging, is pigeon, as to me they taste and cook far better.

Once shot and hung, the bird needs to be plucked. I favour dry plucking to either wet plucking (when it is dipped first in a tank of water) or the method by which it is first dipped into hot wax, then cooled and the feathers removed in big chunks. The reason being is that it keeps the bird dry and firm, and avoids it becoming flabby and bloated. As most game is sold in polystyrene trays and wrapped in plastic film the moisture has nowhere to go. Plucking of all wild game can be a bit tricky, though. You have to take care not to tear the delicate flesh away from the skin. Some are more fiddly than others. With pheasant you need to take it slowly or the flesh will tear around the side of the breast. Pigeon, on the other hand, are really easy and will pluck quickly with no tearing.

All birds are plucked and drawn (gutted) in the same way. I like to keep the livers as they make good pâté (they freeze well). I also keep gizzards and hearts, but you need quite a few to make a proper meal. The only exception to this rule is woodcock. If roasting it, the guts are left in and only removed to make a pâté afterwards (see recipe on page 50). This is possible because a woodcock excretes when it flies, so it should have a clean tract! Once a bird is prepared, I like to chill it well. This also helps if you are going to cut it up or prepare it for various recipes as the flesh is firmer.

PHEASANT

Pheasant are found pretty much everywhere. It's thought they were introduced to the UK by the Romans; the Normans brought more and the rest is history. Nowadays, there are some 40 species, but sadly most are bred for flying not eating! When buying pheasants, look for young, lean birds. Once plucked, and the heads and legs removed, it's difficult to see what you are buying, though hens tend to be smaller and thinner than cock birds. If buying 'feather on' you can identify a female straight away by its light brown plumage. The cock, on the other hand, is beautifully coloured. Tail feathers are a pretty good indication too – short generally means a young bird. A gamekeeper once told me that a good way to tell the age of a cock was by the length of the spur on its leg. A young bird has a short stubby one. An old boy will have a 'Bloody gurt pointed un!'. Beaks will also give you an idea – lower ones that are soft and pliable when squeezed usually indicate young birds. A pheasant will feed two people, one if you're very hungry. Young hen birds lend themselves to being cooked briskly. I like to debone, wrap the breasts in air-dried ham and sauté in butter rather than roast. I also grill them occasionally, but I have never cooked two exactly the same. They are always a bit hit and miss. Older birds I like to braise, make into a pâté or deep fry.

Super-succulent Pheasant Sauté with Soy, Mirin & Ginger

SERVES 4
Preparation: 20 mins
Cooking: 10–12 mins

1 medium egg white

2 teaspoons sesame oil

2 tablespoons cornflour

1 teaspoon salt

½ teaspoon freshly ground black pepper

4 hen pheasant breasts, boned, skinned, sinew removed and cut into 2cm cubes

2 tablespoons olive oil

50g fresh ginger, peeled and finely sliced

1 small onion, finely sliced

4 pak choi, roughly shredded

4 tablespoons mirin

4 tablespoons soy sauce

Velveting is used to keep delicate foods moist and velvety in texture. The food is coated with a mixture of egg white, cornflour and sometimes salt, with either a touch of sesame or vegetable oil. It is then put in the fridge for about 20–30 minutes to ensure that the coating adheres to the food.

1___Put the egg white into a large bowl and break up slightly with a whisk. Add the sesame oil, cornflour, salt and pepper and mix well.

2___Add the cubed pheasant meat and mix well. Cover the bowl with clingfilm and leave to rest in the fridge for 20–30 minutes.

3___Once the meat is rested, heat 1 tablespoon of the olive oil in a wok until smoking. Drain the meat well and fry in small batches for 1–2 minutes just to seal the meat. Remove from the pan and keep warm.

4___Wipe out the wok, then heat the remaining tablespoon of olive oil until smoking. Add the ginger and onion and stir-fry for 2–3 minutes.

5___Add the pak choi and wilt slightly, then return the pheasant to the wok. Add the mirin and soy sauce and cook only briefly to bring all the flavours and textures together – do not overcook!

6___Check the seasoning and serve straight away.

Pheasant Polpettine with Roasted Squash & Pomegranate Molasses

SERVES 4
Preparation: 25 mins,
plus cooling
Cooking: 1–1 ¼ hours

This simple but very effective dish really packs a punch with colour as well as flavour. Any game meat will work here.

SQUASH

1 small butternut squash, skin
  on if small
2–3 tablespoons any oil
salt and freshly ground black
  pepper
sugar, for sprinkling

POLPETTINE

4–5 tablespoons any oil
2 medium onions
2 garlic cloves, crushed
450–500g pheasant meat –
  breast and leg, including skin
  and any of the lovely fat
finely grated zest of 1 small
  unwaxed lemon
2–3 tablespoons dried
  breadcrumbs
2 tablespoons pine nuts,
  lightly toasted
4–5 tablespoons roughly
  chopped fresh parsley
2–3 tablespoons shop-bought
  pomegranate molasses, or
  make your own – see recipe
  below

SQUASH

1___Preheat the oven to 200°C/Gas 6.

2___Cut the squash lengthways into six long slices. Take care as this can be a bit tricky. I tend to: cut it in half, scoop out the seeds with a dessert spoon; lay the cut side flat on the board; and then cut each half into three long slices with the skin left on.

3___Place in a baking tray, drizzle with the oil and lightly dust with salt and pepper and sugar.

4___Roast for 40 minutes or until well browned and cooked through. Remove from the oven and leave to cool. This can be done well in advance.

POLPETTINE

1___Heat 2 tablespoons of the oil in a frying pan and sauté the onions and garlic until they have taken on a little colour. Leave to cool.

2___Whizz the pheasant meat in a food-processor until you have a not too fine purée.

3___Spoon the pheasant into a bowl, add the cooled onions and garlic, lemon zest, breadcrumbs, pine nuts and parsley and mix thoroughly.

4___Slightly wet your hands and then mould the pheasant mixture into small balls roughly the size of a walnut. You will probably end up with around 12.

5___Heat the remaining oil in a large frying pan (ovenproof if transferring to the oven), add the polpettine and brown gently all over. You can cook them right through like this, which will take about 20 minutes. Alternatively, once browned, pop into an oven preheated to 220°C/Gas 7 and cook for 10 minutes.

TO FINISH

1___While the polpettine are cooking, cut the cooked flesh away from the skin of the squash in nice large pieces and warm through in the oven or microwave.

2___Once the polpettine are cooked, add the pomegranate molasses and swirl around the pan so that it coats the meatballs all over. Take care not to burn.

3___To serve, place the warmed squash in the middle of a warm plate and pile the polpettine in the centre.

To make your own pomegranate molasses, put 200ml pomegranate juice into a saucepan, add 2–3 tablespoons caster sugar and gently bubble down to a syrup. Once nice and sticky, remove from the heat and leave to cool slightly, then squeeze in the juice of 1 large lemon and stir.

Grilled Spiced Pheasant
with Mango & Mint Dressing

SERVES 2
Preparation: 20 mins,
plus standing/marinating
Cooking: 16–20 mins,
plus resting

1 pheasant, split in half,
  backbone and all breastbone
  and thigh bones removed
  but leaving the drumsticks
  attached
2 tablespoons good-quality
  mild curry powder
juice of 2 large limes
4 tablespoons olive oil
salt and freshly ground black
  pepper

DRESSING

200ml thick Greek yogurt
1 tablespoon runny honey
1 tablespoon white wine
  vinegar
2 tablespoons chopped fresh
  mint
½ ripe mango, stoned, skinned
  and finely chopped
1 teaspoon ground turmeric

This is a nice way to eat pheasant without too much hassle. Marinating the bird first is very helpful in keeping the meat moist. The dressing is quite a modern twist, but I think it works really well. Just take care not to overcook the bird and to rest it for at least 10 minutes.

1___Mix all the ingredients for the dressing together in a bowl, seasoning with salt and pepper, and leave to stand at room temperature for 30 minutes.

2___Meanwhile, put the prepared pheasant into a glass or ceramic bowl, add the curry powder and rub in well. Add the lime juice, olive oil and salt and pepper and turn to coat well, then cover with clingfilm and leave to marinate at room temperature for 15 minutes.

3___Preheat the grill to its hottest setting and place the pheasant halves on a non-stick baking tray.

4___Cook the pheasant under the hot grill for about 8–10 minutes on each side or until the juices run clear when pierced with a knife or skewer and the bird is nicely glazed. Once nicely browned, you may want to move the pheasant to the bottom of the grill to cook the drumsticks through.

5___Remove the pheasant from the grill, cover loosely with foil and leave to rest in a warm place for at least 10 minutes.

6___Serve hot with the mango and mint dressing spooned over the top.

Popcorn Pheasant with Spicy Dipping Sauce

SERVES 4
Preparation: 40 mins
Cooking: about 20 mins

rapeseed oil, for frying

2 medium pheasant breasts, boned and skinned

3 tablespoons condensed milk

2 tablespoons cold water

2 medium eggs, lightly beaten

salt and freshly ground black pepper

a pinch of chilli powder

½ teaspoon ground cumin

4 tablespoons cornflour

200g fine-ground cornmeal or polenta

DIPPING SAUCE

350ml shop-bought mayonnaise

2 teaspoons roughly chopped fresh red or green chilli

3 teaspoons Dijon mustard

finely grated zest and juice of 1 large unwaxed lime

2 large spring onions, roughly chopped

4 teaspoons chopped gherkins

3 tablespoons chopped fresh tarragon

100g roasted red pepper (jarred are fine), finely chopped

4 tablespoons roughly chopped fresh parsley

4 teaspoons sugar

On the face of it I know it sounds a bit weird adding condensed milk, but trust me it works. I picked up the idea when I was in America, and even using such a small amount really helps the flavour of the finished dish. To me, it's no different than marinating chicken in yogurt to tenderise it. Frying pheasant would never have been entertained when I was a young chef, but I think it does the job of sealing in the juices of this very low-fat bird very well.

1___Pour 2cm rapeseed oil into a frying pan and heat to roughly 175°C.

2___Cut the pheasant breasts into 2cm cubes, removing any sinew from the fillet and inner breast.

3___Combine the condensed milk with the water and eggs in a bowl and season well with the pepper, chilli powder and cumin. Beat together well.

4___Dust the nuggets of pheasant with the cornflour, then drop into the egg mixture and coat well. Repeat the same process with the cornmeal or polenta ensuring the nuggets are coated well.

5___While the oil is heating, mix all the ingredients for the dipping sauce together in a serving bowl, seasoning with salt and pepper.

6___Fry the pheasant in small batches for about 3–4 minutes until golden brown. Drain well, then sprinkle with a little salt.

7___Serve hot with the dipping sauce separately.

Sautéed Pheasant Breasts
with Bacon & Chestnuts

SERVES 2
Preparation: 25 mins,
plus chilling
Cooking: about 40 mins,
plus resting

1 tablespoon olive oil

80g smoked pancetta or
  streaky bacon, cut into 1cm
  cubes

1 medium onion, finely sliced

1 carrot, peeled and finely
  chopped

2 bay leaves

1 teaspoon chopped fresh
  thyme

1 teaspoon crushed garlic

a pinch of ground cinnamon

a pinch of ground cloves

1 tablespoon tomato purée

200ml strong chicken or game
  stock (see page 214)

125ml glass medium-dry white
  wine

salt and ground white pepper

80g vacuum-packed cooked
  peeled whole chestnuts

1 tablespoon cornflour, mixed
  with a little cold water
  (optional)

8 slices of air-dried ham

4 young pheasant breasts,
  boned and any sinew from
  the fillet and inner breast
  removed

25g unsalted butter

In my view, this is the best way to cook pheasant and achieve a consistently good result. The lovely smoky flavour of the bacon and its fat make this simple dish special. Just remember to rest the sautéed breasts for as long as you cook them, and avoid overcooking!

1 Heat the olive oil in a sauté pan, add the pancetta or bacon and cook for about 10 minutes until slightly crisp.

2 Add the onion, carrot, bay leaves, thyme, garlic, cinnamon, cloves, tomato purée, stock, white wine and salt and white pepper to taste. Simmer gently for 20 minutes or until the mixture is reduced to about one-third of its original volume.

3 Add the chestnuts and warm through – be careful, as they will break up if overcooked. Check the seasoning. The sauce should be a silky consistency, so if necessary, add the cornflour mixture (if using) and cook until thickened.

4 Lay the air-dried ham on a chopping board in two lots of four slices, slightly overlapping.

5 Season the pheasant breasts well with salt and pepper, then lay each one inner fillet side up on a set of overlapping ham slices. For each breast, fold in the two opposite sides of the ham, then fold one end over the breast and turn the breast over, carefully wrapping the breast up nice and tightly.

6 Turn the parcels over, ensuring that the 'seam' is now on the underside, and press the ham around the breasts. Chill well for 20 minutes.

7 Heat the butter in a frying pan until it turns slightly brown. Add the parcels 'seam' side up and gently sauté for 2–3 minutes.

8 Carefully turn the breasts over so that the 'seam' is on the underside, leaving the presentation side looking lovely. Sauté again for 2–3 minutes. Remove from the pan, cover loosely with foil and leave to rest in a warm place for a good 10 minutes.

9 Slice each parcel into four or five long slices – the meat should be pink and juicy. Serve with Savoy Cabbage & Onions (see page 218).

Succulent Baked Pheasant Legs
with Black Pudding & Sauerkraut

SERVES 4
Preparation: 25 mins,
plus cooling
Cooking: about 50 mins

150g jarred sauerkraut

16 capers, salted or in brine,
    rinsed and drained

3 pinches of sugar

salt and freshly ground black
    pepper

8 pheasant thighs, boned but
    skin on

8 sheets of filo pastry, trimmed
    to about 23 x 15cm

4 tablespoons melted butter

16 thin slices of good-quality
    black pudding

If overcooked, pheasants can be dry, tough and ghastly, so most chefs use only the breasts and chop the legs up to make the sauce. Cooking the legs this way means you get a second meal out of the bird – save the breasts for a sautéed dish. The use of filo pastry has been overplayed I know, but here I employ buttered filo to hold in the steam so that the legs gently cook, with the butter keeping the pastry crisp.

1___Preheat the oven to 200°C/Gas 6.

2___Spoon the sauerkraut into a saucepan, add the capers and sugar and cook gently for about 10–15 minutes until the moisture has been driven off.

3___Add a good seasoning of salt and pepper and leave to cool.

4___Using a sharp knife, make a few incisions across the skin of each thigh.

5___Lay out two filo pastry rectangles and brush with melted butter. Sit two thighs, skin side down, on the pastry and season well with salt and pepper. Top with two small spoonfuls of the sauerkraut mixture and two slices of black pudding. Season well, then fold up into a nice tight parcel. Repeat with the remaining filo pastry rectangles and thighs.

6___Place the parcels on a large baking tray and brush with melted butter. Season well with salt and pepper and bake for about 35–40 minutes.

7___Serve straight away, with creamed leeks and mashed potatoes.

Spiced Pressed Pheasant & Raisin Terrine with Courgette Pickle

SERVES 12
Preparation : 40 mins, plus cooling, chilling and marinating
Cooking: 1 hour 45 mins, plus about 30 mins for the pickle

10 chicken thighs, boned but skin on
12 pheasant thighs, boned but skin on
salt and freshly ground black pepper
100g raisins, soaked in hot tea for 30 minutes

PICKLE
6 tablespoons olive oil
2 small onions, finely chopped
1 tablespoon cumin seeds
1 tablespoon black mustard seeds
1 tablespoon black onion (nigella or kalonji) seeds
2 teaspoons ground turmeric
4 large courgettes, cut into 1cm cubes
2 garlic cloves, finely chopped
10g good-quality vegetable stock cube, crumbled
100ml white wine vinegar
100ml water
50g sugar

cont'd

Years ago, I had a few chicken thighs left over and wanted to use them make a terrine that was set with their natural jelly. I played around with the idea and it worked really well, so I decided to add game and raisins for a little sweetness. It's a straightforward recipe but with a delicious end result, plus the thighs it uses are the bits that are usually forgotten about. Obviously, it's important that you cook the chicken right through for safety, but that doesn't mean to hell and back, so take care.

PICKLE
1___Heat the olive oil in a small frying pan and sauté the onions in small batches until lightly coloured. Tip into a non-aluminium saucepan.
2___Add the spices to the frying pan and gently toast for 1–2 minutes. Do not burn.
3___Add the toasted spices to the onions along with the courgettes and stir well, then add the rest of the pickle ingredients and mix well.
4___Bring the pickle ingredients to a simmer and cook, uncovered, for 20–25 minutes until almost all the liquid has evaporated and the courgettes are coated in oil. Remove from the heat and season to taste, if necessary.
5___Leave to cool and then chill well, preferably for 1–2 days.

MARINADE
1___Put all the ingredients for the marinade into a glass or ceramic bowl and mix well. Add the thighs with a little salt and pepper and mix well. Cover with clingfilm and leave to marinate in the fridge overnight.

TERRINE
1___Preheat the oven to 150°C/Gas 2.
2___Wet a 10 x 25 x 8cm terrine dish with a little water, then carefully line with a large sheet of clingfilm, leaving plenty overlapping the edges.
3___Remove the thighs from the fridge and put a layer of the chicken ones in the base of the terrine. Drain the raisins and sprinkle a few over the thighs. The next layer should have double the number of pheasant thighs. Repeat, alternating the layers, until the dish is full, then spoon over any remaining marinade.
4___Fold the clingfilm over the top of the terrine and seal well, then press down lightly. Put the lid on and sit in a deep baking tray. Boil a kettleful of water and pour boiling water into the tray until it comes halfway up the sides of the terrine dish. Carefully transfer to the oven and cook for 1 hour 45 minutes.
5___To check if the meat is cooked, lift off the lid and insert a skewer – the juices should run clear.

MARINADE

4 tablespoons soy sauce

2 teaspoons ground cumin

¼ teaspoon chilli powder

200ml dry sherry

2 tablespoons sugar

juice of 2 large lemons

1 tablespoon garam masala

6___Carefully remove the tray from the oven, lift out the dish and remove the lid, then stand the dish on a clean tray. Cover the terrine with a layer of foil, then top with a piece of stiff cardboard, cut to fit the top of the terrine perfectly. Place three or four food cans on top and lightly press down on the card, then leave at room temperature until the terrine has cooled. Chill in the fridge overnight with the card and cans still in place.

7___When ready to eat, remove the cans, card and foil, place the terrine dish in a deep bowl and pour in hot water from the tap so that it reaches 2cm from the top of the dish. Leave for 5 minutes to loosen the sides, then lift the terrine from the dish, remove the clingfilm (there will be a bit of jelly) and slice thickly. Serve with the courgette pickle and some sourdough toast.

PARTRIDGE

Partridge are shot in many places around the world especially South Africa and South America. Red-legged (or French) partridge are very good fliers and can be hard to shoot if there is a fair wind behind them. They're not native to the UK and were probably introduced to these shores in the eighteenth century. They should not be confused with the native English grey partridge. The latter normally fly in coveys (small groups), whereas red-legged fly solo or in groups of up to a dozen or so.

Like pheasant, young birds are preferred to older birds when brisk roasting or sautéing. Legs are soft and pale coloured, and beaks are pliable. I only ever roast English grey partridge, purely because the meat is so tender and delicious. I have never cooked a bad English partridge. Reds are okay grilled, pot roasted and sautéed, but need a little more attention, as they can be very erratic on eating quality. I always serve one bird per person.

Sautéed Partridge
with Cider, Tarragon & Bramley Apple

SERVES 2
Preparation: 20 mins
Cooking: 25 mins

50g unsalted butter, plus another 25g, ice-cold and diced

1 Bramley apple, peeled, cored and cut into 5mm pieces

meat from 2 partridges, including legs and skin, chopped into 2cm pieces

175ml dry cider

¼ x 10g good-quality chicken stock cube, crumbled

2 tablespoons roughly chopped fresh tarragon

a pinch of sugar

salt and freshly ground black pepper

2 teaspoons finely chopped chives

Cider works well with light game meat such as partridge, rabbit or pheasant. The only thickening needed here is a little butter, and provided the liquid has reduced far enough, the butter will emulsify nicely. In cheffy terms, this process is known as *monte au beurre*. The secret, as ever, is not to overcook the partridge.

1___Heat the 50g butter in a non-stick frying pan until slightly golden and bubbling.

2___Add the apple and gently sauté for 2–3 minutes until slightly coloured.

3___Add the partridge and again cook for about 2–3 minutes until just slightly coloured, but do not overcook – the meat should be rose pink when cut open.

4___Remove the apple and partridge from the pan and keep warm.

5___Add the cider and stock cube to the pan and bring to the boil, them simmer until reduced to about half the original volume.

6___Add the tarragon, sugar and salt and pepper to taste.

7___Finally, add the 25g cold butter and swirl through.

8___To serve, place the partridge and apple in deep bowls, pour over the cider mix and sprinkle over the chives.

Pot-roasted Partridges Stuffed with Coconut Rice, Pistachios & Cranberries

SERVES 4
Preparation: 20 mins
Cooking: about 1 hour 30 mins, plus resting

6 tablespoons any oil
2 teaspoons garam masala
½ teaspoon ground cardamom
½ teaspoon ground allspice
½ teaspoon smoked paprika
1 red onion, finely chopped
3 garlic cloves, finely chopped
1 tablespoon peeled and finely chopped fresh ginger
50g ready-to-eat dried apricots, finely chopped
50g dried cranberries, finely chopped
50g dried cherries, finely chopped
250g microwaveable coconut rice, heated
25g honey-roasted cashews, roughly chopped
50g pistachios, roughly chopped
2 tablespoons chopped fresh parsley
salt and freshly ground black pepper
4 partridges
100ml hot chicken stock or water
125ml white wine
50g ice-cold butter, diced

I love pot roasting especially when you have a stuffing like this to bring out the flavours. I normally give it about an hour, then leave it to rest for 20 minutes. There will be just enough juice to make a few lovely spoonfuls of great-tasting sauce. I serve whole birds and let people carve them themselves. A little steamed broccoli or sautéed spinach is all you need to complete the dish.

1___Preheat the oven to 200°C/Gas 6.

2___Heat 3 tablespoons of the oil in a frying pan, add all the spices and quickly fry, stirring, then add the onion, garlic and ginger and cook for 10 minutes until soft.

3___Spoon into a bowl, add the dried fruit, rice, nuts and parsley and mix well. Season with salt and pepper.

4___Stuff the birds with the mixture and tie the legs together with a piece of string. Season with salt and pepper.

5___Heat the remaining oil in a small flameproof casserole dish, add the stuffed birds and fry for 6–8 minutes or until nicely browned.

6___Transfer the casserole dish, without the lid, to the oven and cook for 15 minutes until the birds start to colour.

7___Add the stock or water to the casserole dish, put the lid on and cook for a further 45–50 minutes until the birds are cooked through.

8___Remove the casserole dish from the oven and leave to rest for 20 minutes.

9___Lift the birds out carefully. Boil the juices with the white wine until reduced to about half the original volume. Remove from the heat and whisk in the cold butter to thicken slightly.

10___Serve the birds whole, drizzled with a spoonful of the buttery juices.

Partridge & Yellow Lentil Curry
with Mint & Coriander

SERVES 4
Preparation: 20 mins,
plus soaking
Cooking: about 45 mins

100g dried yellow lentils
4 young red-legged partridges
2 tablespoons vegetable oil
2 small onions, finely chopped
6 garlic cloves, chopped
125g dry-cure streaky bacon
10g good-quality chicken stock
  cube, crumbled
200ml lager
salt and ground black pepper
50g sultanas
a pinch of sugar
250g ripe tomatoes, chopped
10 curry leaves

SPICE MIX
1 tablespoon black mustard
  seeds
1 tablespoon chopped fresh
  red chilli
1 teaspoon ground turmeric
1 teaspoon ground cumin
1 tablespoon black onion
  (nigella or kalonji) seeds
1 tablespoon peeled and finely
  chopped fresh ginger
a pinch of ground asafoetida

TO FINISH
3 tablespoons chopped fresh
  coriander
2 tablespoons chopped fresh
  mint
4 tablespoons double cream

Curry is a real favourite, and in this example I have matched partridge with lentils. They break down and thicken the sauce – provided they have been well soaked. The layers of flavour are also really important here. This treatment will also work for pheasant, duck and goose.

1___Soak the lentils in cold water overnight, then drain.
2___Remove the legs and breasts from each partridge. Chop off the feet and discard. Bone out the thighs and reserve the meat. Leave the drumsticks with the bone in.
3___Cut up both sets of meat into 3–4cm chunks, but keep them separated – this is because the thighs need to cook for a longer period of time.
4___Heat the vegetable oil in a saucepan, add all the spices for the spice mix and cook for a minute or two, but be careful not to burn them.
5___Add the onions, garlic and bacon, **cut into 2cm pieces,** and cook briefly until the onions are slightly softened.
6___Add the partridge thigh meat and drumsticks only and stir to coat in the onion and spice mixture.
7___Add the stock cube, lager, salt and pepper, sultanas, sugar, tomatoes and curry leaves. Bring to the boil and add the lentils, then reduce the heat to a simmer, cover with a lid and cook gently for 30 minutes, stirring occasionally.
8___Drop in the partridge breast meat and stir through, then cook for a further 10 minutes or until the breast is just cooked – do not overcook the breast or it will dry out! By now the sauce should be thick and full of flavour and colour.

TO FINISH
1___Remove the pan from the stove and leave to cool slightly.
2___Season well with salt and pepper and stir in the coriander, mint and cream, then serve with plain boiled rice, natural thick yogurt and chapatis.

Grilled Partridge
with Sweet & Sour Lime & Glass Noodles

SERVES 3
Preparation: 15 mins,
plus marinating
Cooking: about 25 mins

1 small onion, very finely
   sliced
400ml strong cold chicken
   stock
2 tablespoons runny honey
4 teaspoons caster sugar
finely grated zest and juice of 4
   large unwaxed limes
salt and freshly ground black
   pepper
2 partridges
15g unsalted butter
2 tablespoons olive oil
½–1 teaspoon arrowroot or
   cornflour, mixed with a little
   cold water
150g cooked glass (cellophane
   or bean thread) noodles
1 tablespoon olive oil
1 tablespoon toasted sesame
   oil (optional)
1 tablespoon chopped fresh
   coriander

Sometimes with cooking less is definitely more, and here is just such an example of that ethos. The delight of this dish is its simple flavours, put together carefully without detracting from the core ingredient. The noodles also add a straightforward but satisfying element to the dish.

1___Put the onion, cold chicken stock, honey and sugar into a glass or ceramic bowl and mix really well. Add the squeezed lime juice and zest and season well with salt and pepper.

2___Remove the backbone from the each partridge by cutting down either side with a sharp knife. Break open and flatten well, then remove the knuckles.

3___Add the prepared partridge to the stock mixture, cover the bowl with clingfilm and leave to marinate in the fridge overnight, although I have also left it for two days before and it was delicious.

4___When you are ready to cook the partridges, take them out of the liquor and dry them very well with kitchen paper. Season with a little more salt and pepper.

5___Preheat the oven to 200°C/Gas 6.

6___Heat the butter and oil in an ovenproof griddle pan or frying pan over a medium heat. Add the birds skin side down and cook for about 4–5 minutes nice and slowly so that they brown well and evenly, then turn them over and do the same on the other side.

7___Transfer the pan to the oven and roast for about 10 minutes until they are cooked right through, but be careful not to allow them to burn!

8___Meanwhile, pour all the liquor into a saucepan and bring to the boil, then gently simmer until reduced to half its original volume. Check the seasoning and adjust if necessary.

9___Stir in the arrowroot or cornflour mixture and cook until thickened. Blend with a hand blender, or in a standard blender or food-processor, until smooth.

10__Warm the cooked noodles in the olive oil, and sesame oil if using, with the coriander, then serve with the partridge and sauce.

Sautéed Partridge with Roasted Jerusalem Artichokes, Pasta Leaves & Chive Butter Sauce

SERVES 4
**Preparation: 1 hour, plus
cooling, resting and drying
Cooking: about 1 hour 10
mins**

olive oil, for frying
4 partridges, breasts removed
   and thighs boned
salt and freshly ground black
   pepper

ARTICHOKES

2 tablespoons olive oil
250g Jerusalem artichokes,
   washed well and patted dry
4 small sprigs of fresh
   rosemary, bruised with a
   back of a knife
3 tablespoons extra virgin
   olive oil
50g unsalted butter

PASTA DOUGH

120g '00' pasta flour, but white
   bread flour will suffice, plus
   extra for dusting
a pinch of salt
1 tablespoon extra virgin olive
   oil, plus extra for drizzling
1 whole medium egg
1 medium egg yolk

This recipe is a little cheffy and by that I mean somewhat complex, so it does take a bit of time, but it is well worth the effort. Lightly sautéed partridge meat is so delicious and, coupled with a rich butter sauce with the crunch of chive, it is a delight to eat – it sold very well when I had my restaurant. This dish perfectly exemplifies my mantra that great cooking is down to quality ingredients, simply cooked and served. Roasting artichokes intensifies the flavour no end and the flesh takes on a very sweet note that's great with all game.

ARTICHOKES

1___Preheat the oven to 200°C/Gas 6.
2___Put the olive oil in a small baking tray, add the artichokes and rosemary and roll in the oil, then season well with salt and pepper.
3___Roast in the oven for 35–40 minutes, turning occasionally, until very soft and almost bursting, but keep them intact. Remove from the oven and leave to cool.
4___Slice in half lengthways, season the cut sides with salt and pepper and then gently pan-fry in the extra virgin olive oil and butter until they are golden brown, then remove from the pan and keep warm.

PASTA DOUGH

1___Put all the pasta dough ingredients in a food-processor with a dash of water and whizz to a smooth paste. Remove from the machine and knead well on a lightly floured work surface for about 10 minutes until silky in texture. Wrap tightly in clingfilm and leave to rest in the fridge for 20 minutes.
2___Unwrap the pasta dough and knead a couple of times.
3___Set a pasta machine to its widest setting and roll the dough through.
4___Rotate the dough 90 degrees and put through the machine again, then repeat a couple more times so that the dough takes on a nice silky feel.
5___Reduce the setting on the pasta machine gradually so that the pasta is rolled slightly thinner every time you pass it through the machine. Keep going until you have very thin, long strips.
6___Cut the pasta into two or three lengths and hang loose over a long wooden spoon or clean broom handle extending beyond a work surface, secured to the work surface at the other end.
7___Depending on the temperature of the kitchen and also the time of the year, leave the pasta to dry slightly for a few minutes to firm up. But do not allow to completely dry out or you will not be able to cut it without it shattering.
8___Once firm, carefully transfer to a chopping board. Cut into long triangles and place on a tray, flouring lightly to ensure they do not stick together.

SAUCE

50ml dry white wine

50ml white wine vinegar

1 small shallot, very finely
chopped

4 tablespoons whipping cream

150g ice-cold unsalted butter,
diced

4–6 tablespoons finely
chopped fresh chives

SAUCE

1___Put the white wine, vinegar, shallot and salt and pepper into a small saucepan. Bring to the boil, then reduce the heat and simmer until reduced to about a third of the original volume.

2___Add the cream and return to the boil.

3___Remove the pan from the heat and gradually whisk in the cold butter until emulsified. Check the seasoning and adjust if necessary. Keep warm, but not hot or the sauce will split. I find a Thermos flask perfect for this purpose.

TO FINISH

1___Drop the pasta leaves into a large saucepan of boiling salted water one at a time so that they do not stick together and cook for 2 minutes, then drain carefully. Put the pasta in a bowl and drizzle over a little oil to prevent them sticking, then keep warm.

2___Heat a frying pan or wok and add a dash of olive oil. Season the partridge meat well with salt and pepper. Sauté the meat in two batches for a couple of minutes over a high heat, but do not overcook; keep slightly pink.

3___To serve, arrange the cooked artichokes around the outside of a deep bowl. Place the cooked pasta in the centre, overlapping the artichokes slightly. Spoon over the lightly cooked partridge.

4___Stir the chopped chives into the warm butter sauce at the last minute to keep their colour, then spoon a little of the rich sauce over the partridge.

Roasted English Partridge with Chanterelles

SERVES 2
Preparation: 10 mins
Cooking: about 30 mins,
plus resting

25g unsalted butter, plus
    another 25g for sautéeing the
    mushrooms
1 tablespoon vegetable oil
2 English partridges, wishbone
    removed
salt and freshly ground black
    pepper
1 medium shallot, very finely
    chopped
250g small chanterelles,
    cleaned
50g baby spinach leaves

SAUCE
225ml glass medium-dry
    white wine
1 tablespoon white wine
    vinegar
300ml fairly strong game stock
    (see page 214) or chicken
    stock
a pinch of sugar
1 teaspoon ice-cold unsalted
    butter

English partridge is one of my favourite game birds. The flesh is always soft and full of flavour and it really does put the red-legged to shame. However, I rarely cook them these days and prefer to see them flying in small coveys when disturbed. That said, it doesn't mean I won't treat myself occasionally and thoroughly enjoy them. As with woodcock, there really is only one way to cook them and that's simply roasted. Anything else is pure sacrilege in my eyes.

1___Preheat the oven to 220°C/Gas 7.
2___Heat the 25g butter with the oil in an ovenproof frying pan or sauté pan until foaming and a nutty brown colour.
3___Lightly season the birds all over, then add to the pan, each bird one side down, and brown for a minute or so.
4___Transfer the pan to the oven and roast for 5 minutes. Turn each bird onto the other side, spoon over the buttery juices and roast for a further 5 minutes.
5___Turn the birds breast side down, again spoon over the buttery juices and roast for another 3 minutes.
6___Remove the pan from the oven, then place the birds breast side down on a warm plate, cover loosely with foil and leave to rest in a warm place for as long as you cooked them for, so 13 minutes.
7___When the birds have rested, transfer to a chopping board breast side up. First, remove the legs of one bird. Using a sharp knife, slice through the skin where the leg is attached to the breast, then pull the leg back on itself so that the ball and socket joint pops open and carefully pull the leg away.
8___Carefully slice down one side of the breastbone, continuing to cut right along to the wing, then cut through the wing joint. Tease the flesh away from the crown and gently pull the breast meat away. Repeat on the other side.
9___Lay the breast meat on the legs, cover with foil and keep warm while you prepare the other bird, sauce and final ingredients.

SAUCE
1___Roughly chop the carcass up and put into a small saucepan. Add the white wine and vinegar and bring to the boil. Continue boiling until almost all the wine has evaporated.
2___Add the stock and sugar and bring to the boil, then reduce the heat and simmer for about 5–6 minutes until thick and syrupy.
3___Finally, add the cold butter and mix well, then strain through a fine sieve and keep warm and covered.

TO FINISH

1___Heat a small frying pan or sauté pan, add the remaining 25g butter and heat until foaming and just about to change colour.

2___Add the shallot and sauté for 1 minute. Add the chanterelles and toss quickly over a high heat for 2–3 minutes. Season well and spoon into two deep bowls.

3___Wilt the spinach quickly in the hot mushroom pan and add to the bowls.

4___To serve, place the warm partridge legs on top of the mushrooms and spinach, crossed at the top, then place the breasts on top of the legs and carefully spoon over the hot sauce.

Brined Hot-smoked Pheasant or Partridge

Smoking: 30 mins
Steaming: 30 mins

1 brace of pheasant or partridge

BRINE
1 litre chilled water
100g cooking salt

We all know pheasant and partridge have their own distinctive flavours, but brining and smoking most definitely enhances them. The meat will be extremely soft and juicy with a lovely smoky flavour.

1___Mix the cold water and salt together thoroughly in a large, deep strong plastic or stainless steel bowl or container until the salt has dissolved.

2___Put the birds into the brine, ensuring that they are fully immersed, and leave in the fridge for 12 hours or overnight.

3___Remove the birds from the brine and dry thoroughly. I usually do this in my smoker at a temperature of 55°C for about an hour.

4___Then apply a heavy smoke at the same temperature for 30 minutes.

5___Transfer the birds to a steam oven and steam at 82°C until a core temperature of 72°C is reached. Your game is now ready to eat.

Pheasant & Partridge Boudin
with Roasted Shallot & Mushroom

MAKES ABOUT 1.5KG
Preparation: 30 mins

4 shallots, peeled

6–8 chestnut mushrooms

1 tablespoon olive oil, for
   roasting

1kg pheasant or partridge meat

150ml double cream

250ml egg white

20g cooking salt

2g ground white pepper

sausage casings

Olivier Bertho, one of the chefs I supply, asked me to make a boudin blanc for his new menu. He gave me his own recipe for the sausages, and after making them I thought it would be a great way to use game birds. So with Olly's recipe as inspiration, here is my adaptation for pheasant and partridge.

1___Preheat the oven to 200°C/Gas 6.

2___Toss the shallots and mushrooms in olive oil in a roasting tray until well coated, then roast in the oven for 10–15 minutes until caramelised.

3___Remove from the oven and leave to cool.

4___Add the cooled shallots and mushrooms to a food-processor along with all the other ingredients, apart from the casings, and whizz until all ingredients have emulsified together. The mixture should resemble a stiff mousse that is totally smooth in texture.

5___Stuff the mixture into sausage casings and twist into links about 15cm long.

6___Transfer the sausages to a steam oven and steam at 80°C until a core temperature of 70°C is achieved. Alternatively, you can poach the boudin in a saucepan of simmering water for about 20–25 minutes for the same result.

7___Chill the sausages quickly and keep refrigerated until you are ready to use them.

SNIPE

Some say snipe eat better than woodcock. Not in my view, though they are certainly tasty little birds. They are rarely seen on menus, which is shame, but this is probably because they are incredibly difficult to shoot. They fly in a fast, zig-zag fashion and dip and swoop. They love boggy, wet areas and whole days are devoted to shooting them. Once shot, they disappear into the reeds and are so hard to find that even the best gun dogs struggle. They populate many countries in the world, from America to France, Japan to Russia. In the UK, Scotland and the West Country are perfect for snipe shooting. Many arrive from Scandinavia to boost flocks in the winter months.

To make a main meal from these tiny beauties you really need two birds, possibly three per person. They have a delicate flesh and are perfect simply roasted. Even older birds eat really well just roasted.

Pot-roasted Snipe with Smoked Bacon & Chicory

SERVES 2
Preparation: 20 mins
Cooking: about 1 hour 10 mins

200g smoked streaky bacon or pancetta, cubed

4 snipe, drawn and cleaned, heads removed

salt (if needed) and freshly ground black pepper

1 large onion, very finely chopped

4 garlic cloves, finely chopped

2 heads of white chicory (Belgium endive), about 150g total weight, finely shredded

2 teaspoons caster sugar

200ml strong game stock (see page 214) or chicken stock

150ml dry white wine

1 small bunch of watercress roughly chopped

Pot roasting is a great way of keeping in all the moisture to ensure that the end result is delicious. All game is pretty lean, so it makes sense to cook it this way. Chicory is one of my favourite vegetables and often overlooked by chefs. Coupled with bacon and watercress, this not only makes a tasty meal but also a colourful one.

1___Preheat the oven to 220°C/Gas 7.

2___Heat an ovenproof sauté pan with a lid, add the bacon or pancetta and cook until quite crisp and the fat has been rendered. Remove with a slotted spoon and reserve.

3___Season the snipe with pepper only, place breast side down in the hot fat and brown really well. Remove from the pan and reserve with the bacon or pancetta.

4___Add the onion and garlic to the pan and cook over a high heat for about 10 minutes.

5___Add the chicory, pepper, sugar, stock and wine and stir well. Bring to the boil and stir well again, then check the seasoning and adjust if necessary.

6___Stir in the bacon or pancetta and place the browned snipe on top, then cover with a tight-fitting lid, transfer to the oven and cook 40 minutes, basting with the juices occasionally. Do not overcook these delicious birds, otherwise they will dry out and you will lose their delicate flavour.

7___Remove the pan from the oven, then lift the snipe out onto a warm plate, cover loosely with foil and keep warm.

8___Place the pan on the stove and gently cook the chicory, bacon and onion mixture down for about 10 minutes or so until nicely thickened.

9___Stir in the chopped watercress and check the seasoning, adjusting if necessary.

10_To serve, place the birds in warm large bowls with the bacon and chicory stew. All you need are a few buttered boiled new potatoes to accompany.

Roasted Snipe on Sweetcorn & Tarragon Pancakes

SERVES 4
Preparation: 15 mins,
plus cooling
Cooking: about 25–30 mins

4 tablespoons any oil
4 snipe, drawn and cleaned,
   heads removed
salt and freshly ground black
   pepper

PANCAKES
1 medium corn on the cob
3 tablespoons olive oil
½ small onion, roughly
   chopped
1 medium egg, lightly beaten
100g self-raising flour
about 125ml milk
3 tablespoons roughly chopped
   fresh tarragon
oil, for frying

This is another easy dish to prepare and cook, ensuring that the focus is on this magnificent bird. Tarragon goes well with game either in a pancake, stuffing or, in some cases, a light béarnaise sauce.

PANCAKES

1___Stand the corn on its end and, using a sharp knife, carefully slice down to shave off the kernels.

2___Heat 2 tablespoons of the olive oil in a large frying pan or wok. Add the corn kernels and sauté over a high heat for 2–3 minutes until they caramelise slightly. They may 'pop' like popcorn, so be careful. Tip onto a plate.

3___Add the remaining tablespoon of olive oil to the pan and repeat the process with the onion. Spoon onto the plate with the sweetcorn and leave to cool.

4___Mix the egg and half the flour together in a bowl, then gradually whisk in the milk, enough so that the mixture isn't too thin. Add the remaining flour and whisk until you have a smooth batter. Add the tarragon and sweetcorn and onion, then season well with salt and pepper.

5___Heat a little oil in a large non-stick frying pan, then add large spoonfuls of the batter – scoop it up from the base of the bowl so that you get some of the sweetcorn in each spoonful.

6___Cook for 2–3 minutes, then flip over and cook for a further 1–2 minutes until well puffed and slightly browned. Remove from the pan and keep warm. Repeat the process until all the batter is cooked.

SNIPE

1___Preheat the oven to 220°C/Gas 7.

2___Heat the oil in an ovenproof frying pan. Season the snipe all over, then place one side down in the hot oil, transfer to the oven and cook for 5 minutes.

3___At the 5-minute point, remove the pan from oven, turn the birds over onto the other side and return to the oven for a further 5 minutes. Remove from the oven, cover the birds loosely with foil and leave to rest in a warm place for 10 minutes.

4___Transfer the birds to a chopping board and, using a sharp knife, slice through the skin where the leg is attached to the breast, then pull the leg back on itself so that the ball and socket joint pops open and carefully pull the leg away. Carefully slice down one side of the breastbone, continuing to cut right along to the wing, then cut through the wing joint. Tease the flesh away from the crown and gently pull the breast meat away. Repeat on the other side. Cover the meat with foil and keep warm while you repeat with the other three birds.

5___Serve the snipe legs crossed on the warm pancake, with the two tiny breasts on top of the legs.

Roast Snipe with Beet Curry & Crème Fraîche

SERVES 4
Preparation: 20 mins
Cooking: about 35 mins in total, plus resting

4 tablespoons any oil
4 snipe, drawn and cleaned, heads removed
salt and freshly ground black pepper

CURRY
2 tablespoons any oil
½ teaspoon cumin seeds
½ teaspoon black onion (nigella or kalonji) seeds
½ teaspoon ground fenugreek
¼ teaspoon dried chilli with seeds
½ teaspoon ground turmeric
1 red onion, finely chopped
2 garlic cloves, chopped
2 teaspoons tomato purée
200ml game stock (see page 214) or chicken stock
500g cooked beetroot, any colour, cut into 5mm cubes

TO SERVE
150g thick crème fraîche
a few sprigs of fresh coriander

These tiny birds are delicious; Clarissa Dickson Wright reckoned they were tastier than woodcock! They are not often seen on menus these days, possibly because chefs think they aren't worth the trouble. Well yes, I sort of agree with that, but once prepared and cooked they make a fine meal – it just depends on how many you can eat! The sweetness of the beets in this dish offsets the curry spices and crème fraîche. Forget the knife and fork and pick the birds up to eat – all you need is a bib.

CURRY
1___Heat the oil in a saucepan, add all the spices and cook over a low heat for 1–2 minutes.
2___Add the onion and garlic and cook gently for about 4–5 minutes until they start to take on a little colour on the edges.
3___Stir in the tomato purée and stock and bring to the boil, then simmer for 5 minutes or until reduced to roughly half the original volume.
4___Add the beetroot and cook again gently until the stock is well reduced and coating the beets nicely but not too thick. Check the seasoning and adjust if needed.

SNIPE
1___Preheat the oven to 220°C/Gas 7.
2___Heat the oil in an ovenproof frying pan.
3___Season the snipe all over with salt and pepper, then place one side down in the hot oil, transfer to the oven and cook for 5 minutes.
4___At the 5-minute point, remove the pan from oven, turn the birds over onto the other side and return to the oven for a further 5 minutes.
5___Remove the pan from the oven, cover the birds loosely with foil and leave to rest in a warm place for 10 minutes.

TO FINISH
1___Gently reheat the beetroot curry, trying not to break the beets up too much.
2___Remove the pan from the heat, add about 50g of the crème fraîche and swirl through. Keep off the heat.
3___To serve, place the snipe in warm bowls and spoon the curry alongside. Finish with a few sprigs of coriander and a small spoonful of crème fraîche on top of the beetroot.

WOODCOCK

This is probably my favourite game bird. Birds are resident here, but you will hardly ever see them, and for this reason they should only be cooked and eaten by the shooter or his family (I stopped putting them on restaurant menus well over 20 years ago). Many migrate from Scandinavia and Russia and I have heard stories of hundreds resting on oil rigs, as they fly over. They are particularly highly regarded by the French, who pay huge amounts of money for a single bird.

Like snipe they are really hard to shoot as they are always nipping in and out of the tree line, or close to the ground or through hedges. There's no need to hang them as they excrete when they fly. I truss them, though, with their own beaks, as it keeps the breasts nice and plump when roasting, which really is the only way to enjoy woodcock. The flavour and texture is second to none and I have never cooked a tough or flavourless one. Nothing is wasted on a woodcock, even the brain is consumed.

Roast Woodcock

SERVES 1
Preparation: 40 mins
Cooking: about 20 mins, plus resting

1 woodcock, not drawn, head on
50g butter
1 tablespoon any oil
salt and freshly ground black pepper

This is the one and only way I was ever shown how to cook a woodcock, and to me it's the only recipe that comes close to giving this beautiful bird the absolute respect it deserves. Its flesh is like none other, and to be quite frank, any other method of cooking just doesn't do it justice. This recipe is a bit fiddly, but well worth the effort.

1 ___ Preheat the oven to 230°C/Gas 8.

2 ___ Place the woodcock on a chopping board, lying on its breasts. Trim the legs just below the ankles of the bird, for want of a better term.

3 ___ Push the legs back into the body of the bird, making the breasts nice and plump. Scrunch the legs together with a double layer of foil, right down to the bottom of the drumsticks.

4 ___ Heat a small ovenproof frying pan, then add the butter with the oil and heat until foaming and browning slightly. Season the woodcock all over (guts still in) and place one side down in the hot butter and oil, pushing down slightly so that it stays on its side. Carefully transfer the sizzling pan to the oven and roast for 4 minutes.

5 ___ Turn the bird over onto the other side and roast for a further 4 minutes (I use a timer – it's perfect for this). When the 4 minutes is up, turn the bird breast side down for a final 4 minutes of cooking.

6 ___ Remove the pan from the oven, then lift out the bird onto a warm plate, cover loosely with foil and leave to rest in a warm place for 10 minutes.

7 ___ When the bird has rested, transfer to a chopping board. First, cut the head off, cover it with foil and keep warm.

SAUCE

1 small glass full-bodied red
  wine

200ml strong game stock (see
  page 214) or chicken stock

tiny knob (½ teaspoon
  maximum) ice-cold unsalted
  butter

CROUTE

1 slice of white bread

a little extra butter and oil, if
  required

STUFFING

50g unsalted butter

2 small shallots, very finely
  chopped

50ml Armagnac

2 tablespoons fresh white
  breadcrumbs

1 large sprig of watercress, to
  serve

8___Next, remove the legs. Using a sharp knife, slice through the skin where the leg is attached to the breast, then pull the leg back on itself so that the ball and socket joint pops open and carefully pull the leg away.

9___Carefully slice down one side of the breastbone, continuing to cut right along to the wing, then cut through the wing joint. Tease the flesh away from the crown and gently pull the breast meat away. Repeat on the other side.

10___Add the legs and breast meat to the head, cover with foil and keep warm.

SAUCE

1___Chop up the woodcock carcass into small pieces and add to a small saucepan.

2___Add the red wine, bring to the boil and cook rapidly until reduced to half its original volume.

3___Add the stock and let it bubble away while you make the croute.

CROUTE

1___Cut the slice of bread into a large heart shape, discarding the offcuts.

2___Place the frying pan back on the stove and heat gently, then add the bread heart and cook on both sides in the woodcock juices until nice and crisp – you may need to add a little more butter and oil.

3___Remove the croute from the pan and keep warm.

STUFFING

1___Draw the woodcock, removing and throwing away the gizzard. Chop up the heart, liver and intestines.

2___Heat the butter in the frying pan until foaming. Add the shallots and cook over a high heat until they have taken on some colour. Add the chopped innards and sauté for a further minute.

3___Add the Armagnac and then carefully set alight and burn off the alcohol.

4___Add the breadcrumbs and mix to form a loose stuffing.

5___Pack the stuffing onto the croute and keep warm.

TO FINISH

1___The sauce should be nice and thick now, so skim and strain through a fine sieve.

2___Add the tiny piece of butter and swirl through off the heat to thicken and give the sauce a nice sheen.

3___Place the croute in the centre of a warm plate. Cross the woodcock legs and place on top of the croute.

4___Interleave the wing bones on the breasts and place on top.

5___Finally, split the head in two so that you can see the brain and place on top, along with the watercress.

6___Serve with the sauce poured all over.

GROUSE

This wild bird, native to the UK, is found wherever there is plenty of heather – Dartmoor, Exmoor, Wales, northern England and Scotland. Many attempts have been made to rear and release it but never, to my knowledge, successfully. Recent figures suggest that after many years of decline, the population, in some areas at least, is seeing an increase in numbers. This is partly due to good conservation and predator control. Shooting grouse still remains an elite sport and a day's shooting can cost an arm and a leg.

Older birds are great for braising, pâté and broths. Young birds are perfect for simple roasting. I use Clarissa Dickson Wright's test to determine age – if they are young, the plumage will be bright and perfect; older birds tend to shed their toenails in summer and are left with small marks across the nail where the old one has fallen off.

In the UK, the Glorious 12th (August) heralds the opening of the grouse shooting season. Even the young birds still need to be hung for a day or so in my opinion for the flesh to relax. Some would disagree with that, but from a cooking point of view it certainly makes a difference. Towards the end of the season, I tend to hang older birds, depending on weather, for 5–6 days. The flavour of grouse is pretty strong to start with, and hanging can make the taste even stronger, so be careful. With all that in mind, one bird is certainly enough to fulfil even the biggest appetite.

Rustic Grouse Pâté with Port Jelly

SERVES 6–8
Preparation: 40 mins, plus cooling and chilling
Cooking: about 1 hour 50 mins

JELLY

250ml port
10g leaf gelatine, soaked in cold water for 10 minutes to soften

REDUCTION

4 shallots, finely chopped
4 garlic cloves, finely chopped
2 tablespoons finely chopped fresh thyme
½ teaspoon ground allspice
300ml strong game stock (see page 214) or chicken stock
100ml port

Grouse meat has a very distinctive, strong gamey, heathery flavour. Some say that its sacrilege to do anything else with a grouse than plain roasting. I disagree; on the contrary, the meat makes a fabulous pâté as well as great sausages and a nice rich broth or soup. Grouse are expensive, so making a pâté ekes out the meat a little further, plus I make this late on in the season when they are slightly cheaper. Frozen birds are also ideal for this type of preparation.

JELLY

1___If you can, try and make this the day before. Gently heat the port in a small saucepan, but do not simmer or boil. Remove from the heat. Drain and squeeze out the excess water from the softened gelatine, then add to the port and stir until dissolved.

2___Pour into a small dish about 3–4cm deep, cover with clingfilm and chill well until set.

REDUCTION

1___Put all the ingredients for the reduction in a saucepan. Bring to the boil, then reduce the heat and simmer until you have about one-third of the original volume. Leave to cool.

FILLING

8 pigeon breasts, boned,
    skinned and secondary skin
    and sinew removed (see page
    69)
2 large chicken breasts, boned
    and skinned
breast and leg meat from 6
    grouse
14 slices of air-dried ham or
    thinly sliced pork back fat or
    speck
salt and freshly ground black
    pepper

FILLING

1___Preheat the oven to 150°C/Gas 2.

2___Use a meat mincer fitted with an 8mm plate to mince the pigeon, chicken and grouse meat. You don't want a paste, just a nice smooth texture.

3___Put the minced meat in a bowl, add all the cooled reduction and season well with salt and pepper.

4___Wet a 10 x 25 x 8cm terrine dish with a little water and carefully line with a large sheet of clingfilm, leaving plenty overlapping the edges. Then line with the air-dried ham, back fat or speck, overlapping each slice slightly, leaving enough overlapping the dish to cover the top of the pâté.

5___Spoon the filling mixture into the lined dish and press down really well. Fold over the air-dried ham, back fat or speck to cover the top of the pâté. Top with the clingfilm and seal well.

6___Put the lid on and sit in a deep baking tray. Boil a kettleful of water and pour boiling water into the tray until it comes halfway up the sides of the terrine dish. Carefully transfer the tray to the oven and cook for 1 hour 30 minutes.

7___To check if the pâté is cooked, lift off the lid and insert a skewer – the juices should run clear.

8___Carefully remove the tray from the oven, lift out the dish and remove the lid, then stand the dish on a clean tray. Leave the pâté to cool, then top with a piece of stiff cardboard, cut to fit the top of the terrine perfectly. Place a couple of food cans on top and chill in the fridge overnight. If you can, leave the pâté in the fridge for a couple of days to mature.

9___When ready to eat, remove the cans and card, place the dish in a deep bowl and pour in hot water from the tap so that it reaches 2cm from the top of the dish. Leave for 5 minutes, then lift out, turn upside down and gently pull the clingfilm – the pâté should fall out easily with a little tug.

10__Unwrap the pâté and place on a clean board, as you will have a lot of juice and jelly from the 'cook out'.

11__Turn the jelly out and cut into nice small cubes. Serve the pâté in thick slices with the jelly on the side. Some crisp sourdough toast with plenty of cold butter is all you need as accompaniment.

Easy Grouse Soup
with Rice Noodles & Beef Marrow

SERVES 4
Preparation: 40 mins
Cooking: about 1 hour 10 mins

2 tablespoons any oil

4 grouse, legs removed and
chopped; breasts removed,
skin on; carcasses roughly
chopped

750ml game stock (see page
214) or chicken stock

2 garlic cloves, chopped

1 tablespoon finely chopped
fresh red chilli

1 small leek, split, washed well
and finely chopped

1 small onion, finely sliced

1 red pepper, deseeded and
finely chopped

100g very thin dried rice
noodles

100g button mushrooms,
finely sliced

salt and freshly ground black
pepper

marrow from 1kg middle-cut
thigh beef bones

100g Iceberg lettuce, finely
shredded

2 tablespoons roughly chopped
fresh coriander

Easy it is, but this does take a little preparation time. The secret is to keep everything nice and simple, leaving the strong flavours to come to the fore themselves. The other thing to stress here is that the grouse must be pink – gently poach this fabulous meat for a few seconds only. Marrow bones are getting easier to find nowadays, partly due to being featured on television programmes and used by top chefs. I have just come back from Atlanta, Georgia, where even a burger chain is offering a half-cut roasted marrow bone as a side. A butcher will sell or split the bones for you so that you can remove the marrow. Bear in mind that the colder the marrow, the easier it is to remove. The silkiness that the marrow gives to the soup is amazing!

1___Heat a large non-stick frying pan, add the oil and the chopped leg meat from the grouse, along with the carcass, and gently fry for a good 10 minutes to brown really well. Pop into a large saucepan, add the stock and bring to the boil, then reduce the heat and gently simmer for 35–40 minutes.

2___Skim the oil and any bits from the surface. Strain well, discarding the cooked bones, return to the washed-out saucepan and skim again.

3___Add the garlic, chilli, leek, onion and red pepper and bring to the boil, then reduce the heat and simmer for 15 minutes or until the vegetables are just cooked.

4___Add the rice noodles and mushrooms and then simmer just until the noodles have softened – this will not take long, seconds probably. The flavour will now be really developed and the liquid slightly reduced, so you may have to add a little water if the soup is getting too thick. Season well with salt and pepper.

5___Slice the grouse breasts lengthways into thin strips, about 5mm wide, and cut the marrow into 2cm cubes.

6___When ready to serve, reheat the soup. Drop in the lettuce and grouse and just warm – do not overcook.

7___Finally, add the marrow and coriander and leave for 1 minute, then quickly serve in warm deep bowls.

Potted Grouse & Wild Duck with Spiced Pears

SERVES 6–8
Preparation: about 1 hour,
plus marinating, cooling
and chilling
Cooking: about 4 ¾ hours

12 wild duck legs

1 large glass Madeira

100g sea salt

4 tablespoons chopped fresh
thyme, plus 2 teaspoons
finely chopped

12 black peppercorns, crushed

400g pork back fat, thinly
sliced, plus another 400g,
unsliced and very cold

500g duck or goose fat

2 large chicken breasts, boned
and skinned

4 grouse breasts, boned,
skinned and secondary skin
and sinew removed

300ml strong duck stock or
game stock (see page 214)

4 shallots, finely chopped

3 garlic cloves, finely chopped

1 large smoked duck breast,
boned and skinned

salt and freshly ground black
pepper

sugar, for seasoning

2 pinches of ground mace

a pinch of ground cinnamon

300g unsalted butter

4 tablespoons chopped fresh
parsley

Potting meat was traditionally a great way of preserving food. It basically meant placing cooked meats in lots of fat and setting it to keep out the air. The large amount of fat coupled with the salt kept the bugs at bay. Nowadays we have refrigeration, which negates the use of too much fat, or even salt for that matter, but it's still a nice way to serve game. I also 'pot' pigeon, venison, rabbit and hare. Due to the rather rich nature of this dish, it needs an accompaniment that will cut the richness, and spiced pears are the perfect answer. This recipe is quite involved and therefore takes a bit of time to prepare and cook, but it really is well worth the effort. It's also a good way to use up wild duck legs that normally get thrown in the stock pot. Serve the spiced pears with any potted meat.

1___The day before, place the duck legs in a glass, ceramic or stainless steel dish. Cover with the Madeira, sea salt, the 4 tablespoons thyme and crushed peppercorns and rub in well. Cover with clingfilm and leave in the fridge for 12 hours, turning occasionally.

2___The next day, preheat the oven to 150°C/Gas 2.

3___Line an 18 x 9cm soufflé dish with the thinly sliced back fat, leaving enough overlapping the dish to cover the top of the dish.

4___Wash the duck legs well under cold water and pat dry with kitchen paper.

5___Heat the duck or goose fat in an ovenproof pan until hot but not sizzling. Place the duck legs in the hot fat and cover with foil.

6___Transfer the pan to the oven and cook for about 2 hours until the legs are soft and succulent.

7___Remove from the oven and leave the duck legs to cool in the fat to room temperature.

8___Meanwhile, use a meat mincer fitted with a 5mm plate to mince the very cold back fat quickly. Then mince the chicken and grouse and mix with the minced back fat.

9___Heat the duck or game stock in a saucepan, add the shallots and garlic and cook down until you have a thickish glaze, then strain out the garlic and shallots and leave to cool.

10__Meanwhile, rinse the duck legs under a warm tap to remove the excess fat and then pull the flesh off into smallish chunks, discarding the skin and bones.

11__Cut the smoked duck breast into roughly 2cm pieces.

12__Add the cooled stock to the minced chicken, grouse and back fat and mix well. Season well with salt and pepper and sugar.

13__Add the mace, cinnamon and the remaining 2 teaspoons thyme and mix well, then finally add the smoked duck breast pieces and duck leg meat. Do not overmix. It's best to overseason slightly at this point, as the dish will lose some of the seasoning once cooked and chilled.

PEARS

4 ripe Williams or Bon
  Chretien pears
350ml cold water
juice of 2 large lemons
300g caster sugar
6 cloves
1 cinnamon stick
4 pinches of ground mixed
  spice

14__Spoon the mixture into the lined soufflé dish and pack down well. Cover the top of the mixture with the overlapping back fat, then a double layer of foil.

15__Sit the soufflé dish in a deep baking tray. Boil a kettleful of water and pour boiling water into the tray until it comes halfway up the sides of the dish. Carefully transfer the tray to the oven and cook for about 2 hours 30 minutes.

16__To check if cooked, insert a skewer into the centre of the meat – the juices should run clear.

17__Carefully remove the tray from the oven, lift out the dish and stand on a clean tray. Place a saucer on top and sit a bag of flour in it to lightly press the potted meat. Leave to cool, then chill in the fridge overnight.

18__When chilled, slice off the top of the potted meat to make it even, then wrap around the sides with a double layer of foil and secure well.

19__Melt the butter very gently so that you end up with pure clear butter and whey, then spoon the clear butter into a bowl and keep warm, adding the chopped parsley and a little pepper.

20__Pour onto the potted meat, ensuring that you cover the top entirely, then carefully place in the fridge to chill well.

PEARS

1___Carefully peel the pears and cut into five long wedges. Remove the core and trim off the long end slightly so that you end up with nicely shaped pieces.

2___Bring the water and lemon juice to the boil in a saucepan with the sugar and spices, add the pears and cover with greaseproof paper. Top with a saucer to keep them suspended in the syrup.

3___Simmer for 1 minute, no more, then remove the pan from the heat and leave to cool completely.

4___Cover and chill well.

5___To serve, remove the foil from the potted meat, cut a large wedge and serve with walnut toast, a little lightly dressed salad and the spiced pears.

Roast Grouse with Spiced Pear
& Sweet Potato Ketchup

SERVES 4
Preparation: 15 mins
Cooking: 15–20 mins,
plus resting

Like grey partridge, grouse requires very little effort, and in my book it has such an intense flavour that a powerful accompaniment like ketchup works very well indeed. The ketchup recipe does make a lot, but it will keep in the fridge for ages.

KETCHUP

250g soft, ripe pears (any variety will do, but they need to be very ripe), peeled, halved, cored and chopped

100ml cider vinegar

100ml water

½ teaspoon ground allspice

½ teaspoon ground cloves

2 x 10g good-quality vegetable stock cubes, crumbled

50ml olive oil

75g muscovado sugar

250g sweet potato, peeled and very finely chopped

1 tablespoon cornflour, mixed with a little cold water

salt and freshly ground black pepper

GROUSE

50g unsalted butter

2 tablespoons any oil

4 young grouse

KETCHUP

1___Put the pears in a saucepan with the vinegar, 100ml water, spices, stock cubes, olive oil and sugar and cook for about 15 minutes until they become a light pulp.

2___Cook the sweet potato in a saucepan of boiling water for 30 minutes until very soft and overcooked. Drain well.

3___Add the sweet potato to the cooked pears, just cover with water and cook for a further 15 minutes. Whizz in a blender or food-processor to a fine sauce/purée. Return to the pan.

4___Stir in the cornflour mixture and cook until thickened, seasoning well with salt and pepper. The end result should resemble thick double cream.

GROUSE

1___Preheat the oven to 220°C/Gas 7.

2___Heat the butter with the oil in an ovenproof frying pan until foaming and a nutty brown colour. Season the grouse inside and out, then add to the pan, each bird one side down, and cook for 1 minute until browned.

3___Transfer the pan to the oven and roast for 5 minutes. Turn each bird onto the other side, spoon over the buttery juices and roast for a further 5 minutes. Finally, turn the birds breast up, again spoon over the buttery juices and roast for another 5 minutes.

4___Remove the pan from the oven, then place the birds breast side down on a warm plate, cover loosely with foil and leave to rest in a warm place for 15 minutes.

5___Transfer the birds to a chopping board and, using a sharp knife, slice through the skin where the leg is attached to the breast, then pull the leg back on itself so that the ball and socket joint pops open and carefully pull the leg away.

8___Carefully slice down one side of the breastbone, continuing to cut right along to the wing, then cut through the wing joint. Tease the flesh away from the crown and gently pull the breast meat away – the meat will be nice and pink. Repeat on the other side.

9___Cover the legs and breast meat with foil and keep warm while you repeat with the other three birds.

10_To serve, cross two legs on a warm plate, then lay the two breasts on top, with a small bowl of the ketchup on the side – simple and to the point.

PIGEON

The scourge of farmers the world over – a good sized flock can decimate a field of young peas in an hour! Most of the time you only see a few at a time, but when the farmers are sowing or harvesting, thousands will turn up from nowhere. Another good time to shoot them is when nearly ripe barley or corn has been flattened by a freak summer shower or storm. They will be all over it like flies.

But put all of that to one side and you can eat really well with a plump, young pigeon. Pigeon is extremely cheap (probably the cheapest of all game meat) and it has a good proportion of fine flavoured breast meat. Many dishes can be made from this pest. It's the easiest of all birds to pluck and it normally takes a couple of minutes, without tearing. I generally never hang them, as I don't think it improves the flavour; if anything, it can spoil it. They lend themselves to brisk roasting, sautéing in butter, plus they make excellent soups and pâté or terrines.

If roasting whole, one is normally served per person. I serve three breasts per person, so getting two portions out of three birds. The bones make excellent stock.

Hot-smoked Twiggies

MAKES 1KG
Preparation: 30–40 mins
Drying: 10 days

700g pigeon meat
300g wild boar belly (ordinary belly pork will do if you cannot get boar)
20g curing salt (containing 0.6% sodium nitrite)
2g ground white pepper
1g ground nutmeg
2g ground caraway
sheep casings

Although these delicious little sausages are cooked, they can be kept without refrigeration. They are great to have in your pocket as a snack when you are out in the countryside pursuing your favourite country sport.

1___Use a meat mincer fitted with an 8mm plate to mince the pigeon and boar.

2___Put the minced meat into a large bowl, add the salt and spices and mix together thoroughly with your hands.

3___Stuff the mixture into sheep casings and twist into 15–20cm links.

4___Place in a smoker on sticks, equally spaced, and hot smoke until a core temperature of 72°C is reached.

5___Hang the sausages first in a warm environment for 12 hours, and then in an environment with a temperature of 12–15°C and a relative humidity of about 78 per cent with little airflow – a cellar or pantry would work well – for about 10 days or until they have lost 10–15 per cent in weight. The sausages are now shelf stable and do not need refrigeration.

Roast Pigeon Breasts with Cassis

SERVES 4
Preparation: 15 mins
Cooking: about 1 ½ hours

4 pigeons, carcasses and legs
    removed and reserved
2 tablespoons vegetable oil
salt and freshly ground black
    pepper

STOCK/SAUCE

2 tablespoons vegetable oil,
    plus a little extra for cooking
    the pigeon
1 carrot, peeled and finely
    chopped
1 small onion, finely chopped
1 celery stick, finely chopped
½ small leek, split, washed
    well and finely chopped
2 garlic cloves, crushed
2 tablespoon red wine vinegar
100ml red wine
about 500ml well-flavoured
    game stock (see page 214) or
    chicken stock
2 bay leaves
a sprig of fresh rosemary
a sprig of fresh thyme
1 teaspoon tomato purée
6 juniper berries, crushed
a few black peppercorns
4–5 tablespoons crème de cassis
50g frozen blackcurrants,
    defrosted, juice reserved
10g ice-cold unsalted butter
    or 2 teaspoons double cream
    (optional)

Wild pigeon meat is delicious to eat and extremely good value for money. Older pigeons are better braised or stewed, while younger birds are great just roasted very quickly and eaten pink. The meat is quite rich, so therefore they need a little acidity such as blackcurrants to balance the richness. This recipe looks complicated, but it really is quite simple. The hardest part is the shopping, as there are several ingredients in the stock, but these are essential to achieve a full-flavoured finished sauce. The stock also makes a great broth or winter soup.

STOCK

1___Preheat the oven to 220°C/Gas 7.

2___Chop up all the pigeon carcasses and legs, place them in a roasting tray and then roast for about 20 minutes until lightly browned. Alternatively, you can gently sauté the bones for 12–15 minutes to achieve pretty much the same effect as roasting them.

3___On the hob, add the oil to the tray, then the vegetables and garlic and lightly brown over a medium heat, but do not allow to burn.

4___Add the vinegar and red wine and bring to the boil, scraping all the little browned bits from the base of the pan where the bones have stuck – this gives the stock a little extra flavour and colour. Cook down until almost all the liquid has evaporated.

5___When all the stuck bits have been loosened, add the stock and bring to the boil, then reduce the heat to a gentle simmer.

6___After 5 minutes, skim really well, then add the herbs, tomato purée, juniper berries and peppercorns. Continue to simmer for 30–40 minutes, skimming all the time.

7___Strain well, then transfer to a clean saucepan and simmer until you have a well-reduced and syrupy stock – do not over-reduce, otherwise the stock will taste like Marmite. Strain well once more through a fine sieve.

PIGEON

1___Preheat the oven to 220°C/Gas 7.

2___Heat the vegetable oil in an ovenproof frying pan.

3___Season the pigeon crowns well inside and out with salt and pepper, then place one breast side down in the hot oil and cook until lightly browned.

4___Turn onto the other breast and then transfer the pan to the oven and roast for 15 minutes.

5___Remove the pan from the oven, cover loosely with foil and leave to rest in a warm place for 5 minutes.

SAUCE

1___Meanwhile, reheat the stock, adding the cassis, and stir well.

2___Season with salt and pepper and warm through again, then add most of the blackcurrants and juice. At this point the sauce must not boil, otherwise the fruit will break up.

3___Cover and keep warm. You can swirl in the unsalted butter here to give the sauce a nice gloss or, if you really want to show off, add the cream to lighten the sauce slightly.

TO SERVE

1___Using a sharp knife, slice the pigeon from the crown along the backbone, keeping as close to it as possible, then carve away from the breastbone. Repeat with the other side of the crown, leaving 8 small breasts. They should be beautifully pink.

2___Carve each breast into three or four long slices.

3___Serve on warm plates or bowls with a little of the sauce and the remaining blackcurrants, along with wilted spinach and small cubes of potato roasted with a little garlic and rosemary.

Pigeon, Chicken, Parsley & Pea Pie

SERVES 4–6
Preparation: 25 mins, plus cooling and chilling
Cooking: about 1 hour 20 mins, plus standing

2 large chicken legs

1 bay leaf

about 500ml strong chicken or game stock (see page 214)

about 10 black peppercorns

salt and freshly ground black pepper

1–2 tablespoons vegetable oil

1 large onion, finely chopped

50g unsalted butter, very soft

40g plain flour

115g frozen peas, defrosted but drained well

2 x 28cm shortcrust pastry discs, 450g total weight

8–10 pigeon breasts, boned, skinned and secondary skin and sinew removed (see page 69), chopped into 1cm pieces

4 tablespoons roughly chopped fresh parsley

beaten egg, for glazing

Not your normal pigeon pie, this version uses a velouté – a thickened sauce made with stock rather than milk. If you can, try and make the filling the day before and chill it really well. Not only does it fill the pie more easily but I think the pastry cooks more evenly. You could use sautéed pigeon breasts if you prefer, or at least fry them for a minute or two to get a little colour.

1__Put the chicken legs, bay leaf, stock and peppercorns into a saucepan and bring to the boil. Skim off any scum, season with salt and simmer gently for 30 minutes.

2__Meanwhile, heat the oil in a frying pan, add the onion and cook gently until softened, then reserve.

4__When the chicken has cooked, remove it from the stock and leave to cool slightly, reserving the stock.

5__Take the skin off the chicken and remove the flesh from the bones, then cut the meat into large chunks.

6__Strain the chicken stock through a sieve into a measuring jug – you will need 400ml of poaching liquid. Pour the measured stock into a clean saucepan and bring to the boil.

7__Mix the soft butter and flour together to form a paste. Reduce the heat so that the stock is simmering and gradually whisk in the butter and flour paste. The sauce will thicken as it returns to the boil and it should be of a 'dropping' consistency, which means a spoonful of the sauce should take about 2 seconds to drop off a wooden spoon once it's turned onto its side. If the sauce is too thin, the pie won't hold its shape, but if it's too thick, that's awful as well!

8__Add the chunks of chicken, peas and cooked onion to the sauce, and season well. Leave the sauce to cool and then chill well so that it thickens.

9__Preheat the oven to 180°C/Gas 4.

10__Line a 23cm round, 4cm deep, loose-bottomed flan tin with one disc of pastry, leaving the excess pastry overhanging the edge.

11__Stir in the chopped pigeon breasts and parsley to the pie mix, then spoon into the flan case and spread out evenly.

12__Moisten the top edge of the pastry with a little cold water, then lay the other disc of pastry over the top and pinch the edges together to seal. Trim, then brush the top with beaten egg and make a small incision in the centre to let out the steam.

13__Bake for 40 minutes or until golden brown and cooked through. Once cooked, it's best to leave the pie to stand for about 20 minutes so that it is easier to cut. It won't then scald your mouth either!

Potted Pigeon & Wild Duck

SERVES 6–8
Preparation: 35 mins,
plus cooling and chilling
Cooking: about 2 hour
40 mins

400g pork back fat, thinly
 sliced, plus 300g, unsliced,
 very cold
2 large chicken breasts, boned
 and skinned
8 pigeon breasts, boned,
 skinned and secondary skin
 and sinew removed
 (see page 69)
500ml strong duck or chicken
 stock
4 shallots, finely chopped
3 garlic cloves, finely chopped
1 large smoked duck breast,
 boned and skinned
4 wild duck breasts, boned,
 skinned and secondary skin
 and sinew removed
salt and freshly ground black
 pepper
sugar, for seasoning
2 pinches of ground mace
a pinch of ground cinnamon
2 teaspoons finely chopped
 fresh thyme
300g unsalted butter
4 tablespoons chopped fresh
 parsley

Pigeon is perfect for potting as it has a very fine flavour. The slightly fattier wild duck is an ideal partner for it, and the deep flavour you end up with makes a delicious starter or main course. One of my chefs once described it as 'posh man's pork pie'.

1___Preheat the oven to 150°C/Gas 2 and line an 18 x 9cm soufflé dish with the thinly sliced back fat, leaving enough overlapping the dish to cover the top of the dish.

2___Use a meat mincer fitted with an 8mm plate to mince the very cold back fat quickly. Then mince the chicken and pigeon and mix with the minced back fat.

3___Heat the duck or chicken stock in a saucepan, add the shallots and garlic and cook down until you have a thickish glaze, then strain out the garlic and shallots and leave to cool.

4___Meanwhile, cut the smoked duck breast and wild duck breasts into roughly 2cm pieces.

5___Add the cooled stock to the minced chicken, pigeon and back fat and mix well. Season well with salt and pepper and sugar. Add the mace, cinnamon and thyme and mix well, then finally add the smoked duck breast and wild duck meat. Do not overmix. It's best to overseason slightly at this point, as the dish will lose some of the seasoning once cooked and chilled.

6___Spoon the mixture into the lined soufflé dish and pack down well. Cover the top of the mixture with the overlapping back fat, then a double layer of foil.

7___Sit the soufflé dish in a deep baking tray. Boil a kettleful of water and pour boiling water into the tray until it comes halfway up the sides of the dish. Carefully transfer the tray to the oven and cook for about 2 hours 30 minutes. To check if cooked, insert a skewer into the centre of the meat – the juices should run clear.

8___Carefully remove the tray from the oven, lift out the dish and stand on a clean tray. Place a saucer on top and sit a bag of flour in it to lightly press the potted meat. Leave to cool, then chill in the fridge overnight.

9___When chilled, slice off the top of the potted meat to make it even, then wrap around the sides with a double layer of foil and secure well.

10_Melt the butter very gently so that you end up with pure clear butter and whey, then spoon the clear butter into a bowl and keep warm, adding the chopped parsley and a little pepper.

11_Pour onto the potted meat, ensuring that you cover the top entirely, then carefully place in the fridge to chill well.

12_To serve, remove the foil, cut a large wedge and serve with thickly-buttered toast and a little redcurrant jelly on the side.

Spiced Pigeon Sauté with Green Lentils & Lime

SERVES 4
Preparation: 30 mins
Cooking: 40 mins

½ teaspoon ground cumin

½ teaspoon ground coriander

salt and freshly ground black
  pepper

12 pigeon breasts, boned,
  skinned and secondary skin
  and sinew removed (see
  recipe introduction)

4 tablespoons any oil, plus
  another 4 tablespoons

1 large onion, finely chopped

1 small carrot, peeled and
  finely chopped

2 celery sticks, finely chopped

2 garlic cloves, finely chopped

500ml well-flavoured game
  stock (see page 214) or
  chicken stock

1 tablespoon tomato purée

juice of 1 large lime

100g dried red lentils

2 heaped tablespoons chopped
  fresh basil

100g dried green lentils

100g thick Greek yogurt

4 tablespoons roughly
  chopped fresh parsley

Pigeon breasts, as with all birds, have two skins – the outer, feathered one and a fine, almost transparent one that also covers the silver sinew running to one end of the breast. If these are removed, it makes a big difference to the eating experience. I tend to remove them in a similar way to skinning a fillet of fish: on a board and with a knife at a 45-degree angle to the board, pulling the skin as you carefully slice it away.

You need to end up with a thickish stew here, so I have said to use 500ml stock, but you may have to keep an eye on this – you can always add a little more liquid, but you can't remove it successfully. Bear in mind that the red lentils will thicken up the stew considerably. Pigeon meat can take a fair bit of spice in my view, so don't be shy.

1___Mix the spices together well, adding pepper at this stage but leaving the salt to later, then sprinkle over the pigeon breasts. Leave until ready to cook.

2___Heat the 4 tablespoons oil in a saucepan, add the vegetables and garlic and cook for 10 minutes over a high heat to get a little colour.

3___Add the stock, tomato purée, lime juice, red lentils and basil and bring to the boil. Season well with salt and pepper, then reduce the heat and simmer for about 15 minutes until all the vegetables and lentils are cooked.

4___Meanwhile, place the green lentils in a saucepan of cold water and bring to the boil. Add a little salt and then simmer for 10 minutes until just tender but not mushy. Drain and refresh in cold water and set aside.

5___Once the stew is cooked, carefully spoon it into a blender and whizz until very smooth – it will probably need two or three goes. You want a thick stew broth that is not too runny. Re-season well and add the cooked green lentils.

6___When ready to serve, heat the remaining 4 tablespoons oil in a large non-stick frying pan.

7___Season the spiced breasts well with salt, then add them to the hot oil and sauté for 2–3 minutes on each side, making sure they are nice and pink. Remove the pan from the heat and leave the pigeon to rest for 5 minutes. .

8___Heat the thick stew and spoon into the middle of warm deep bowls.

9___Slice the breasts lengthways and drain well on kitchen paper, then lay over the stew.

10__Stir the yogurt well to make it nice and soft, then spoon a good blob in the centre of the stew and sautéed pigeon. Scatter with the chopped parsley and serve.

Steamed Pigeon & Wild Rabbit Pudding

SERVES 4–6
Preparation: 40 mins,
plus chilling and cooling
Cooking: 2 hours 45 mins

PASTRY

280g self-raising flour, plus
extra for dusting

140g shredded beef suet, at
room temperature (which
helps to make a smoother
pastry)

a pinch of salt

freshly ground black pepper

2 tablespoons chopped fresh
parsley

1 medium egg, beaten

50g melted butter, for greasing

This very simple pudding is bursting with flavour and texture interest. The thing to remember is to remove all traces of secondary skin and what we call silver skin (sinew), a membrane you will find in the pigeon fillet on the inside of the breast once it's removed from the bone, and also towards the wing joint in the breast. It can also be found in the rabbit meat lining the backbone just under the skin. The same applies to wild boar, hare and all deer. It's completely inedible even when cooked for a long time, so must be removed. Suet crust is perfect for this type of pudding, as it holds in gravies and juices well. I add an egg to help bind the pastry together and I also use self-raising flour, again to add a little more structure and lightness to the end result.

PASTRY

1___Put the self-raising flour into the bowl of an electric mixer fitted with a dough hook.

2___Add the suet, salt, pepper and parsley and mix together well on a slow speed.

3___Mix in beaten egg and enough cold water to make a soft but not sticky dough.

4___Remove the dough from the mixer, lightly flour and knead for a minute or two, but don't go mad and overwork the gluten. Work the dough quickly, as the raising agents will be working away and the dough will start to rise.

FILLING

1___While the pastry is chilling, cut the rabbit and pigeon into 2cm pieces and put into a bowl.

2___Put the garlic, onion, thyme, redcurrant jelly, red wine, Worcestershire sauce and salt and pepper into a separate bowl and really whisk well together.

3___Put the plain flour into a small bowl, add a little of the cold water and mix to a smooth paste, then add the rest of the water and mix well.

4___Whisk the flour mixture into the red wine mixture.

5___Place a steamer on the stove and fill the base with boiling water.

6___Heat a large frying pan, add the oil and then the bacon and cook until nicely browned, almost crisp. Remove from the pan and leave to cool.

7___Add the pigeon in small batches and cook until slightly coloured. Add to the bacon.

8___Repeat with the rabbit, again adding to the bacon and pigeon. Leave to cool.

FILLING

200g saddle of rabbit from 1 medium-sized rabbit, free of secondary skin and sinew (see recipe introduction)

250g pigeon breast meat from plump wood pigeons, free of secondary skin and sinew (see recipe introduction and page 69)

2 garlic cloves, crushed

1 small onion, finely chopped

1 tablespoon chopped fresh thyme

1 tablespoon redcurrant jelly

150ml red wine

2 tablespoons Worcestershire sauce

salt and freshly ground black pepper

40g plain flour

about 100ml cold water

2 tablespoons any oil

200g dry-cure English back bacon, cut into 1cm pieces or cubes

250ml game stock (see page 214) or pigeon stock

PUDDING

1___Lightly butter a 17cm Pyrex bowl 10cm deep, or equivalent receptacle.

2___Remove the pastry from the fridge and lightly dust a board with flour.

3___Cut off about a quarter of the dough and reserve. Roll out the rest of the dough and carefully use to line the bowl, ensuring that the dough overhangs the rim of the bowl by 2–3cm.

4___Spoon half the meats into the lined bowl and add half the onion and wine mixture.

5___Add the rest of the meat, then the rest of the onion mixture and top with the rest of the meat. Pour over the stock but do not overfill.

6___Moisten the top edge of the pastry with a little cold water. Roll out the reserved dough into a disc slightly larger than the top of the bowl.

7___Lay the disc of pastry over the top of the bowl, then press the edges together with your thumb to seal and fold the excess pastry over so that the top edge of the bowl is clean and the pudding is well sealed.

8___Make a very small incision in the centre of the pudding to let the steam out. Cover with lightly oiled foil and secure well.

9___Place the bowl in the steamer, cover with a tight-fitting lid and steam for 2 hours 30 minutes, topping up with boiling water every 40 minutes or so.

TO FINISH

1___Once the pudding is cooked, remove from the steamer and place on a board.

2___Remove the foil and place a plate on top of the pudding. Carefully turn the bowl over onto the plate and then gently lift off the bowl, and hey presto!!

3___Serve with a little game gravy (see page 217), mashed potatoes and roasted parsnips.

Sautéed Pigeon Breasts
with Red Wine Butter Sauce & Chorizo Mash

SERVES 4
Preparation: 20 mins,
plus chilling
Cooking: about 40 mins,
plus resting

½ medium egg white

2 tablespoons cornflour or
   arrowroot

1 tablespoon olive oil, plus
   another 6 tablespoons for
   cooking the pigeon

a pinch of salt

12 pigeon breasts, boned,
   skinned and secondary skin
   and sinew removed (see page
   69)

MASH

500g potatoes, such as
   Marfona, White King Edward
   or Wilja

50g butter or 4 tablespoons
   olive oil

about 100ml hot milk

2 small soft cooking chorizo,
   about 200g total weight,
   skinned and cut into 5mm
   cubes

SAUCE

3 tablespoons red wine or
   balsamic vinegar

1 small glass full-bodied
   red wine

2 shallots, very finely chopped

100g ice-cold butter, diced

salt and freshly ground black
   pepper

Coating the pigeon breasts in egg white and starch makes the meat tender and succulent. The soft cooking chorizo turns the mash into a meal in itself, and works well with the pigeon. Red wine butter sauce is slightly over the top, but does add another taste profile.

PIGEON

1___Whisk the egg white and cornflour or arrowroot together well in a shallow dish. Add the 1 tablespoon olive oil and salt, then whisk again.

2___Add the whole pigeon breasts and mix well to coat. Cover the dish with clingfilm and chill for 20 minutes.

MASH

1___Peel and cut the potatoes into regular pieces. Put the potatoes in a saucepan of water and bring to the boil, then reduce to a simmer for 12–15 minutes until they are cooked through. Drain well and leave in a colander to steam dry for 5 minutes.

2___Add the butter or olive oil and mash well or push through a ricer. Whisk in enough hot milk to get a soft but not runny mash – it should not be too creamy. Keep warm.

3___Heat a non-stick frying pan, add the chorizo and cook until the fat runs. Then add to the mash and stir in. Keep covered and warm – it will look great.

SAUCE

1___Put the vinegar, red wine, shallots and a pinch of salt and pepper into a saucepan Bring to the boil, then cook down until you have 2–3 tablespoons left.

2___Remove the pan from the heat and add the cold butter, whisking all the time. The sauce will thicken naturally; do not boil. Check the seasoning and adjust if necessary. Keep covered and warm.

TO FINISH

1___Heat a large frying pan and add the 6 tablespoons olive oil.

2___Carefully lift the pigeon breasts out of the bowl and remove most of the starch and egg white coating. Sauté in the hot oil for 2 minutes, then turn over for a further minute or two. Transfer the pigeon to a warm plate, cover loosely with foil and leave to rest in a warm place for 10 minutes. Do not overcook – the pigeon needs to be nice and pink still when sliced.

3___When ready to serve, slice the breasts on a long angle. For each serving, place a large spoon of mash in the centre of a warm deep bowl. Top with three sliced pigeon breasts and a good spoonful of sauce.

QUAIL

Quail are found pretty much everywhere but numbers are dwindling and I have to say I have never seen a wild one here in the UK. Nowadays most quail you see for sale will have been farmed.

This tiny bird can be cooked in a variety of ways – roasted, poached, grilled, barbequed, made into pâté – all of them really nice. It's also a meat that almost any flavour profile can be attached to. Leaf through cookery books or browse the internet and you will see recipes from India, Africa, the Far East, Europe, America and the Caribbean, which is testament to its versatility. I have never plucked one, but being small it's probably more fiddly than hard.

Pot-roasted Quail with Warm Aubergine & Pomegranate Salad

SERVES 2
Preparation: 20 mins
Cooking: about 45 mins

3 tablespoons olive oil

4 large quails

salt and freshly ground black pepper

1 onion, very finely chopped

2 garlic cloves, finely chopped or crushed

4 tablespoons aubergine pickle

1 small aubergine, cut into small cubes

1–2 sprigs of fresh sage

100ml water

10g good-quality chicken stock cube, crumbled

2 tablespoons chopped fresh mint

2 large plum tomatoes chopped

2 small Little Gem lettuces, roughly chopped

seeds from 1 large pomegranate

The mix of cooked aubergines and lettuce here makes a very nice warm salad. Any juices from the quail while pot roasting are also absorbed by the salad. I tend to pot roast a lot of game due to the fact that the flesh, whether bird or meat, is very lean, thereby ensuring that the end result stays moist and tasty.

1___Preheat the oven to 180°C/Gas 4.

2___Heat the olive oil in a heavy-based flameproof casserole dish.

3___Season the birds all over with salt and pepper, add to the hot oil and brown all over. Remove from the pan and reserve.

4___Add the onion and garlic and cook for 3–5 minutes until they have taken on a little colour.

5___Add the pickle, aubergine and sage, stir well and cook 5 minutes.

6___Stir in the water and stock cube, and season well with pepper.

7___Bring to the boil, then place the quails on top of the stew. Cover with the lid, transfer to the oven and cook for 30 minutes.

8___Remove the casserole from the oven. Lift out the quails onto a warm plate, cover loosely with foil and keep warm.

9___Place the pan back on the stove and gently cook the aubergine mixture to thicken slightly.

10_Remove from the heat, add the mint, tomatoes, lettuce and pomegranate seeds and mix well.

11_Re-season and then serve the warm salad with the cooked quails.

Grilled Quails with Syrup Glaze
& Minted Broad Beans

SERVES 4
Preparation: 45 mins,
plus marinating
Cooking: 15 mins

4 plump quails
salt and freshly ground black
   pepper
2 tablespoons vegetable oil
about 450g podded broad beans
2 tablespoons chopped fresh
   mint
a pinch of caster sugar
2 tablespoons olive oil

MARINADE
2 tablespoons good-quality
   maple syrup
1 tablespoon soy sauce
½ teaspoon dry English
   mustard powder
2 tablespoons strong chicken
   stock
1 teaspoon sherry vinegar

This sounds like an odd combination but it works well. I once prepared a salad whilst working in Italy with these ingredients and the locals loved it. A word of caution though – if you're using the large, late season broad beans, peel them from their outer skins, as they can be bitter. If using very young or frozen baby beans (which I love) they will be fine.

1___Place a quail breast side up on a chopping board.

2___Using a sharp knife, insert the knife into the cavity and run it up to the neck of the bird. With the knife blade just one side of the spine, gently slice through the back of the bird.

3___Use your hands to break the breastbone of the quail so that it flattens nicely.

4___Lay the quail on the breast so that the cavity is uppermost and cut away the spine and discard.

5___Repeat with the other three quails.

6___Mix all the ingredients for the marinade together in a glass or metallic bowl.

7___Add the opened quails to the marinade and really coat them well with the marinade. Cover the bowl with clingfilm and leave to marinate in the fridge for 1–24 hours, stirring occasionally.

8___Lift the quails from the marinade and pat dry with kitchen paper. Season well with salt and pepper.

9___Heat the vegetable oil in a frying pan or griddle pan, add the quails skin side down and cook over a medium-high heat for about 4–5 minutes until nicely browned. Turn over and cook on the other side for about 4–5 minutes until cooked through but not dry and stringy. Take care, otherwise the birds will burn, and keep basting all the time with the marinade. Sometimes I cook these small birds under the grill instead – it's up to you.

10__Remove from the heat, cover loosely with foil and leave to rest in a warm place for 10 minutes.

11__Meanwhile, add the beans to a saucepan of rapidly boiling salted water and just bring back to the boil.

12__Immediately remove the pan from the stove, strain the beans through a sieve or colander and then refresh under cold water. Pop the beans out of their bitter skins.

13__Mix the beans with the mint, sugar, salt and pepper and the olive oil in a bowl. Keep at room temperature.

14__To serve, place a small spoonful of the beans in the centre of each warm plate and top with a quail. The best way to eat the bird is to pick it up with your fingers and tuck in.

Grilled Marinated Quails
with Crispy Parsnips & Walnut Oil

SERVES 4
Preparation: 20 mins, plus marinating
Cooking: about 20 mins, plus resting

4 large quails
2 small parsnips
sunflower or safflower oil
salt and freshly ground black
  pepper

MARINADE
1 tablespoon runny honey
2 star anise, lightly crushed
4 cardamom pods, crushed
2 tablespoons finely chopped
  fresh mint
2 tablespoons any vinegar
juice of 1 large lime
1 lemongrass stalk, bruised,
  or 1 tablespoon good-quality
  lemongrass paste
4 tablespoons extra virgin
  olive oil
1 tablespoon peeled and finely
  chopped fresh ginger
2 garlic cloves, finely chopped

SALAD
80g mixed salad leaves – I
  like lamb's lettuce with
  watercress and a few
  mustard greens, but choose
  any you like
10 cherry tomatoes, halved
1 tablespoon sesame seeds,
  lightly toasted
2 tablespoons walnut oil
1 tablespoon any vinegar

Quail meat is very good for latching flavours onto; anything goes. But a word of caution: take care not to overcook or the meat, as with all game, tends to dry out. The marinade is a very potent one, and the longer you can leave these cute birds in it, the better. Walnut oil was all the rage in the eighties and consequently vastly overused. But I still really like the flavour and the little used here makes a good addition to the finished dish.

1__Place a quail breast side up on a chopping board. Using a sharp knife, insert the blade into the cavity and run it up to the neck of the bird. With the blade just one side of the spine, gently slice through the back of the birds.

2__Use your hands to break the breastbone of the quail so that it flattens nicely. Lay the quail on the breast so that the cavity is uppermost and cut away the spine and discard. Repeat with the other three quails.

3__Mix all the ingredients for the marinade together in a bowl, adding a touch of salt and pepper. Add the opened quails and really coat them well. Cover the bowl with clingfilm and leave to marinate in the fridge for a couple of hours, though 20 minutes will do at a pinch.

4__Meanwhile, peel the parsnips and then, using a Japanese mandolin or shaving very thinly with a sharp knife, cut into thin slivers. Spread out on a tray and leave for 20 minutes so that they are dry to the touch and will crisp up more quickly when fried.

5__Heat the oil in a deep-fat fryer or deep saucepan to 175°C and fry the parsnips in small batches for 2–4 minutes until crisp and lightly coloured. Drain well and season with a little salt. Keep warm but do not cover.

6__Preheat the grill on a medium setting.

7__Remove the quails from the marinade and place on a baking tray. Season well with salt and pepper. Grill skin side up for 4–5 minutes, then turn over and cook for a further 4–5 minutes, leaving the flesh slightly pink. Cover loosely with foil and leave to rest in a warm place for 10 minutes.

8__Place all the ingredients for the salad, apart from the oil and vinegar, in a large bowl and mix well.

9__When ready to serve, add the oil and vinegar to the salad and season well with salt and pepper. Pile the salad into the centre of each plate, top with the grilled quails and then the parsnip chips and serve straightaway.

Thai Quail & Crab

SERVES 4
Preparation: 30 mins
Cooking: about 20 mins

salt and freshly ground black
  pepper
250g fine green beans
350g small broccoli florets
25g unsalted butter
2 tablespoons olive oil
4 large quails
2 heads of pak choi
200g fresh crabmeat (claw
  meat)
1 small bunch fresh coriander

DRESSING
50ml sunflower oil
40g palm sugar
finely grated zest and juice and
  from 2 large unwaxed limes
1 tablespoon toasted sesame
  oil
1 tablespoon peeled and very
  finely chopped fresh ginger
2 garlic cloves, finely chopped
¼ teaspoon dried chilli flakes

I had a dish very similar to this while filming in Vietnam; the combination of warm, cold, raw and cooked is really nice. The matching of shellfish and meats is normal in the Far East and the pungent, sweet dressing brings all the ingredients together. Just remember to slightly undercook the quail and it will be delicious.

1___Preheat the oven to 220°C/Gas 7.

2___Bring a large saucepan of salted water to the boil. Plunge in the beans and cook for 2 minutes, then remove with a slotted spoon and refresh in iced water.

3___Repeat the process with the broccoli, using the same boiling water.

4___Once both vegetables are cooled, drain them really well.

5___Heat the butter with the oil in an ovenproof frying pan until foaming. Season the quails well, then place breast side down in the hot butter and oil and cook for 2–3 minutes until nicely browned.

6___Transfer the pan to the oven and roast for 10 minutes. Turn the birds over and roast for a further 3 minutes.

7___Remove the pan from the oven, cover the birds loosely with foil and leave to rest in a warm place for at least 10 minutes.

8___Meanwhile, make the dressing by placing all the ingredients in a bowl, adding salt and pepper and whisking well – that's it.

9___To serve, rip the leaves from the pak choi and wash well, then drain and dry on kitchen paper. Arrange the pak choi on four large plates. Add the beans and broccoli, then sprinkle over the crabmeat and coriander .

10__When the birds have rested, transfer to a chopping board. Using a sharp knife, slice through the skin where the leg is attached to the breast, then pull the leg back on itself so that the ball and socket joint pops open and carefully pull the leg away.

11__Carefully slice down one side of the breastbone, continuing to cut right along to the wing, then cut through the wing joint. Tease the flesh away from the crown and gently pull the breast meat away. Repeat on the other side.

12__Cut each breast into two nice pieces, and cut the legs in half through the joint. Cover the legs and breast meat with foil and keep warm while you repeat with the other three birds.

13__Arrange the warm quail meat over the vegetables, crabmeat and coriander. Finally, spoon over the dressing and serve.

Ostrich Braise with Paprika, Caraway & Potatoes

SERVES 4
Preparation: 20 mins
Cooking: 30–35 mins

½ medium egg white

1 tablespoon cornflour, arrowroot or tapioca flour

a pinch of salt

a pinch of freshly ground black pepper

1 tablespoon olive oil

400g ostrich breast, sliced into 2cm strips

2 tablespoons any oil, plus extra if needed

SAUCE

2 tablespoons any oil

1 large onion, thinly sliced

4 garlic cloves, crushed

1 teaspoon caraway seeds

400g can chopped tomatoes

1 teaspoon sugar

2 tablespoons any vinegar

10g good-quality chicken stock cube, crumbled

2 medium potatoes, cut into roughly 2cm cubes (no need to peel)

2 heaped teaspoons smoked paprika

salt and freshly ground black pepper

TO SERVE

soured cream

smoked paprika

chopped fresh parsley

Like a lot of game, as it's so lean ostrich can take very little time to cook. So here again I employ the clever velveting technique (see also page 15), which involves coating the meat in starch and egg white to seal in the moisture. Whilst on a filming trip to Namibia I had quite a lot of ostrich, and the chef on the game reserve taught me that you must under- or very carefully cook this incredibly lean meat. Again like a lot of game meat, especially from Africa, it's so good for you, being very low in saturated fat. This recipe has a two-stage process: a nice thick potato and tomato braise, with quickly sautéed ostrich added at the very last moment.

SAUCE

1___Heat the oil in a saucepan, add the onion, garlic and caraway seeds and sauté for 3–4 minutes to allow the onion to take on a little colour and soften slightly.

2___Add the tomatoes, sugar, vinegar, stock cube, potatoes and smoked paprika, and stir well.

3___Add enough water just to cover the mixture, then season with a little salt and pepper, bearing in mind that the stock cube will cook out and you can adjust the seasoning later.

4___Bring to the boil, then reduce the heat and gently simmer for about 15 minutes until the potatoes are cooked.

OSTRICH

1___Meanwhile, whisk the egg white, cornflour, the arrowroot or tapioca, and the salt, pepper and olive oil together well in a bowl.

2___Add the ostrich strips and really mix well.

3___Once the potatoes are cooked, heat the oil in a wok or large frying pan, add the ostrich strips in small batches, making sure they are not stuck together, and sauté briskly until well sealed and half-cooked – you may need a touch more oil for the later batches – then remove with a slotted spoon.

TO FINISH

1___Once the ostrich strips have been seared, stir them into the hot tomato braise and leave for 10 minutes to cook the ostrich through off the heat. Do not overcook.

2___Serve with soured cream, a little more smoked paprika and lots of chopped parsley.

2   GROUND GAME

Ground Game

Probably the most common, and widely consumed, ground game is deer, known as venison. Other species, such as wild boar, rabbit and hare are not as popular. When I was in my early twenties, I worked for a butcher that specialised in game, where we spent most of our time working on wild venison. We would receive culled carcasses from all over the country and, once they'd been skinned, we would butcher them into primal cuts that eventually went for export. A certain amount was prepared and sold in London for the hotel trade, but back then it was rare to see venison, or indeed any game, on supermarket shelves. We also dealt with an abundance of rabbit and hare, but, again, most was destined for export and sold 'in skin', which is something you don't see these days. If we fast forward to today, game of all kinds is available in our shops. For many farmers, deer farming has proved a successful way of diversifying and several of our big parks manage herds in a similar way to farming. In my opinion, the venison from these sources is of a superior and more consistent quality to wild venison. The culling of the latter is done for conservation reasons; the meat it provides is a by-product. Tighter regulation, however, is gradually replacing our rather antiquated game laws and as a result there has been an upturn in the quality of wild venison offered for sale.

Rabbits have also been successfully farmed, both here and on the Continent, and are a little milder in flavour than their wild cousins. Wild boar was the food of our ancestors and was hunted relentlessly. It is now making a comeback in our forests, albeit with a little human help. The brown hare, which, incidentally, has never been domesticated or farmed, is perhaps the least popular ground game, though the meat is wonderful. Hopefully the recipes Phil has written will inspire people to eat a bit more of it . *Simon*

VENISON

In the past, venison was not available to the masses; it was hunted for sport by the rich and noble and poached relentlessly by the poor for food (at the cost of their lives if caught). The last ten years or so, however, have seen venison's popularity surge and it is increasingly stocked by both butchers and supermarkets. With healthy eating and heart disease becoming more common, it slots in nicely as a red meat alternative with low cholesterol and little fat, and the fact that national parks and many farmers have turned to deer for an alternative form of income has meant that top quality venison is available in greater quantities. The recipes that Phil has written reflect a totally modern approach to this genre of game cookery and, once tried, venison will become a welcome addition to the weekly shopping bag. *Simon*

Rich Venison Sauce with Pappardelle

SERVES 4
Preparation: 20 mins
Cooking: about 1 hour

4 tablespoons olive oil

2 medium onions, finely chopped

2 garlic cloves, finely chopped

500g minced venison

300ml red wine or port

1 teaspoon dried oregano

2 tablespoons tomato purée

10g good-quality beef stock cube, crumbled

300ml strong game stock (see page 214) or chicken stock

400g can chopped tomatoes in juice

4 tablespoons cold water

2 teaspoons cornflour, mixed with the water

salt and freshly ground black pepper

500g cooked pappardelle pasta

Pappardelle pasta is made for big, rich and delicious sauces like this. Once the meat is nicely browned, just simmer gently until you have a wonderfully coloured deep-flavoured sauce. Don't rush it – just let it simmer away. It's that simple!

1___Heat the olive oil in a saucepan, add the onions and garlic and cook for 10 minutes until slightly browned.

2___Add the mince and break up well with a wooden spoon. Then cook over a high heat for a few minutes, stirring well, until all the moisture has evaporated and the meat and veg are starting to brown well.

3___Add the red wine or port and reduce right the way down until you have only about one-third of the original volume.

4___Next, add the oregano, tomato purée, beef stock cube, stock, tomatoes and their juice and water, bring to a simmer and cook gently for 35–40 minutes.

5___Stir in the cornflour mixture and cook until slightly thickened, then season well with salt and pepper.

6___Serve spooned over the warm pappardelle.

Hunter's Breakfast

SERVES 2
Preparation: 15 mins
Cooking: 10 mins

1 small very fresh Roe deer
liver (although any deer liver
will suffice), cleaned well and
rinsed, then soaked in cold
water overnight in the fridge)
70–100g unsalted butter or
dripping
salt and freshly ground black
pepper
3 tablespoons plain flour
(optional)
4 slices of thick sourdough
bread, cut on a long angle
4 free-range game bird eggs –
any sort will do; see recipe
introduction for suggestions
2 tablespoons Gentleman's
Relish or something similar

After an early morning, there really is only one breakfast to eat, the Hunter's Breakfast. All deer livers have a fine flavour and texture; I think they are far superior to veal or calves' liver. The fresh livers need to be cleaned and rinsed well in plenty of cold water. You will find that the liver holds a fair amount of blood if very fresh, so a good soaking is essential to remove all traces. Once that's done, I very rarely remove the translucent skin, especially if the animal is young. Just slice, pat dry and cook lightly, avoiding overcooking – pink or rose is perfect. Game bird eggs are also good fun to cook, so I sometimes serve my liver with fried pheasant or duck eggs, or even turkey or pigeon eggs – it's really up to what you fancy and can find. My daughter Winnie and I love this breakfast, although she likes baked beans with hers, which is fair enough.

1___Drain the liver, then slice and remove any large tubes. Pat dry with kitchen paper.

2___Heat 70g butter or dripping in a large frying pan until foaming and slightly browning.

3___Season the liver slices well with salt and pepper. Dust with the flour if you like – this really is optional.

4___Sauté the liver very quickly in the butter for about 30 seconds on each side, ensuring that you leave it pink. Remove from the pan and keep warm.

5___Add the bread slices to the pan and cook in the buttery/fatty juices until crunchy and well browned; you may need to add the extra butter or dripping. Remove from the pan and keep warm.

6___Finally, fry the eggs in the pan and season well.

7___To serve, spread a very thin smear of relish onto the slices of bread and top with the eggs, with the liver on the side.

Rich Venison Stew
with Prunes, Chestnuts & Juniper

SERVES 4
Preparation: 25 mins
Cooking: about 2–2 hours 20 mins, plus cooling

4 tablespoons vegetable oil or beef dripping, plus a little extra for browning the veg

750g boneless stewing venison, shoulder is best, cut into 5cm cubes

salt and freshly ground black pepper

350g salt pork, cut into 5cm cubes to match the venison

2 large red onions, roughly chopped

2 carrots, peeled and cut into small cubes

4 garlic cloves, crushed

3 tablespoons plain flour

1 heaped tablespoon tomato purée

300ml full-bodied dry red wine

560ml strong beef stock

10 juniper berries, crushed

2 sprigs of fresh rosemary

3 bay leaves

2 tablespoons runny honey

12 ready-to-eat prunes, pitted

50g pine nuts, lightly toasted

15 frozen or vacuum-packed cooked peeled chestnuts

4 tablespoons chopped fresh parsley

Venison makes a great winter main course in the form of this full-flavoured, beautifully rich casserole or braise. It's the sort of dish that when you come in from the cold makes you immediately salivate. Being such a rich meat, a little venison goes a long way, so don't be surprised if you feed six from this. A lot of people find the meat a bit too strong and rich, but I think half the problem with venison is the way you cook it, and what you cook it with. Venison is a very lean beast with hardly any fat, which is fine when cooking the saddle or loin chops, but when it comes to the slower-cooked cuts, do take care that the meat is gently cooked or it will dry out and toughen very quickly indeed. A chef I used to work for said to me 'always cook venison with respect', and how true that is.

I would always use fresh, wild venison, but the farmed and frozen cuts are perfectly acceptable; just ensure that they are defrosted and dried well on kitchen paper before you cook them, otherwise they will boil rather than fry in the pan. The balance of the sweetness from the prunes and the pungency of the juniper and herbs is ideal with venison, and the chestnuts make a perfect pairing. This stew can also be steamed in suet crust (see page 70) for the most gorgeous steamed pudding and mash.

1___Preheat the oven to 160°C/Gas 3.

2___Heat the vegetable oil or dripping in a large frying pan.

3___Season the venison well with salt and pepper, add to the hot oil or dripping and brown well, then remove from the pan to a deep flameproof casserole dish. You may need to do this in a couple of batches to avoid overloading the pan.

4___Season the salt pork with pepper only and brown in the same way, then remove from the pan and add to the venison.

5___Add a touch more oil to the pan, add the onions, carrots and garlic and cook for about 8–10 minutes until they have a nice brown and caramelised colour to them. Remove from the pan and reserve.

6___Return the browned meats to the pan, add the flour and tomato purée and mix well. I think it's good to let the flour catch a little, as it adds flavour and colour to the whole stew.

7___Stir in the red wine and the beef stock and bring to the boil, slowly, stirring well.

8___When just simmering, add the juniper, rosemary and bay leaves.

9___Next, add the honey, prunes and pine nuts, and season well with salt and pepper.

10__Cover with a tight-fitting lid, transfer to the oven and cook for 1 hour and 15 minutes. The stew must cook very slowly in the oven, otherwise it will dry out and toughen – this is a very important point. You will notice a wonderful smell all around the kitchen and the house, juniper, venison, bay and rosemary everywhere.

11__Remove very carefully from the oven and take off the lid. The aroma will be fantastic. Check that the meat is soft and juicy; it should fall apart when gently squeezed. If it's still a little tough, then pop back into the oven for a further 20–30 minutes.

12__Once the meat is cooked, stir in the chestnuts, re-cover and return to the oven for another 15–20 minutes to warm the nuts through. Do not overcook the nuts or they will fall apart.

13__When the stew is finally cooked, remove from the oven and leave to cool for a good 30 minutes, covered. If the stew is too hot, you really cannot eat or enjoy it. Stir in the chopped parsley.

14__The best way to serve this dish is to just pop the whole thing in the middle of the table and let people help themselves. A large bowl of lightly cooked broccoli tossed in a little unsalted butter and a bowl of mash are all you need with this and, of course, a large glass of Shiraz.

Venison Patties with Prune & Herb Salad

SERVES 4
Preparation: 20 mins
Cooking: 15 mins

8 venison sausages

2 spring onions, finely
chopped

4 ready-to-eat prunes, pitted
and finely chopped

1 teaspoon chopped fresh
thyme

salt and freshly ground black
pepper

olive oil, for cooking and
drizzling

2 ciabatta rolls

1 garlic clove, cut in half

SALAD

2 tablespoons chopped fresh
flatleaf parsley

2 tablespoons fresh chives
roughly sliced on the
diagonal

2 tablespoons chopped fresh
coriander leaves

2 spring onions, finely
shredded

8 ready-to-eat prunes, pitted
and chopped

1 tablespoon sesame seeds,
toasted

2 tablespoons red wine vinegar

4 tablespoons extra virgin
olive oil

salted butter, to serve

Here is a very simple way of turning venison sausages into something a little different. Most supermarkets now stock them or, better still, you could seek out a local butcher who makes his own. Yes, the prunes really do work well with venison, and also hare.

1___Preheat the oven to 200°C/Gas 6 and put an ovenproof frying pan in the oven to heat.

2___Split the skin of each sausage, throw away the casings and place the meat in a bowl. Add the spring onions, prunes, thyme and salt and pepper.

3___Mix together with your hands and then shape into eight even-sized patties.

4___Transfer the heated frying pan from the oven to the stove, add a thin film of olive oil and then quickly sear the venison patties on both sides. Return to the oven and cook for a further 5–6 minutes or until cooked through and tender. Do not overcook or they will dry out too much.

5___Heat a griddle pan until hot. Split the ciabatta rolls, drizzle with a little olive oil and rub with the cut sides of the garlic. Griddle until nicely marked.

SALAD

1___Put the herbs in a bowl, add all the other ingredients for the salad and mix well to combine.

TO SERVE

1___Place the bottom halves of the ciabatta rolls on warm plates and top each one with a nice knifeful of salted butter, then with a venison patty.

2___Pile the salad on top and place the top halves of the rolls to the side.

Venison Ham

MAKES 1KG
SERVES 6–8
Smoking: 30 mins

1 haunch of Muntjac or
   Chinese water deer, bone in
   or boneless

BRINE
1.5 litres hot water
500g black treacle
240g curing salt (containing
   0.6% sodium nitrite)
5g sodium ascorbate

I first made this ham about ten years ago with the haunch from a Muntjac deer and used the same method as I would to make a ham from a pork leg. But this turned out to be quite salty and really not very nice, so I decided to make it with a much weaker brine and added some black treacle. The result I have to say was quite amazing.

1   Put the hot water into a large, deep strong plastic or stainless steel bowl or container, add the black treacle and mix until dissolved.

2   Stir in the curing salt until dissolved, then add the sodium ascorbate.

3   Chill the brine and then immerse the haunch in it, ensuring that it is completely covered.

4   Leave in the fridge for ten days.

5   Remove the haunch from the brine and dry thoroughly. I usually do this in my smoker at a temperature of 60°C for about an hour.

6   Place in smoker and apply a light smoke for about 30 minutes at a temperature of 55°C.

7   Transfer the ham to a steam oven and steam at 78°C until a core temperature of 68°C is reached.

Venison Bresaola

MAKES 1KG
Drying: 3–4 weeks

1kg venison loin, preferably
from a Red or Fallow deer,
completely free of gristle and
sinew
fibrous casing (man-made
casing derived from
collagen), for wrapping the
bresaola

DRY CURE
25g curing salt (containing
0.6% sodium nitrite)
3g dextrose
2g sodium ascorbate

This is an adaptation of the Italian classic, which is traditionally made with beef and is dry cured with salt and herbs and spices. I use venison loin here and leave out the herbs and spices because I like the venison flavour to speak for itself.

1___Mix the dry cure ingredients together thoroughly and apply to the venison.
2___Put into a strong plastic container and refrigerate for a week, turning over after 3 days.
3___Remove the venison from the container and wash off with lukewarm water.
4___Wrap the venison in the fibrous casing.
5___Hang the venison in an environment with a temperature of 12–14°C and a relative humidity of about 70–75 per cent with little airflow – a cellar or pantry would work well – until it is quite firm to the touch, when it is ready to eat. This will typically take about 3–4 weeks.
6___Slice wafer thin to serve.

Roast Venison Loin
with Blackcurrants & Shredded Leeks

SERVES 4
Preparation: 20 mins
Cooking: about 15 mins,
plus 10 mins for the leeks

2 tablespoons olive oil

4 x 200g pieces of venison loin
– Roe, Fallow, Red or Sika or
small antelope or springbok

salt and freshly ground black
pepper

SAUCE

300ml red wine

600ml strong venison or game
stock (see page 214)

6 tablespoons crème de cassis

200g frozen blackcurrants,
defrosted

10g ice-cold unsalted butter

LEEKS

2 large leeks

50g unsalted butter

2 tablespoons extra virgin
olive oil, plus a little extra (or
butter) to serve

½ x 10g good-quality vegetable
stock cube, crumbled

freshly ground black pepper

2 tablespoons white wine or
water

Loin is probably the best cut for roasting or sautéeing. Not just venison – small antelope or springbok would also be ideal. It cooks in minutes, so seal it well and cook for the shortest time possible, then leave it in a warm place to finish cooking. If you overcook it, it will be dry and stringy. A well-reduced game stock is essential for the small amount of sauce you are serving here. It's almost a seasoning with a big flavour punch. I use frozen blackcurrants as the freezing process breaks down the cell structure, allowing more flavour and giving a brilliant colour to the sauce.

LEEKS

1___Slice each leek in half from top to bottom, leaving the whole thing attached at the root end. Turn and slice each half in half again so that you end up with four pieces attached at the root. Wash, slice as thinly as possible, discard ends and drain well.

2___Heat the butter with the olive oil in a sauté pan until the bubbling subsides, then add the leeks and stir well. Add the stock cube, pepper and wine or water and cook over a high heat until the leeks just start to soften. Then spoon into a colander.

3___These can be made in advance and chilled, then warmed in a microwave or sauté pan with a little oil or unsalted butter when ready to serve.

VENISON

1___Preheat the oven to 220°C/Gas 7.

2___Heat the olive oil in an ovenproof frying pan. Season the loins well, add to the hot oil, brown well on both sides, then transfer to the oven and roast for 5–6 minutes.

3___Remove the pan from the oven, then transfer the venison to a warm plate, cover loosely with foil and leave to rest in a warm place for 6–8 minutes.

SAUCE

1___While the meat rests, tip away any oil from the frying pan, then add the wine and boil rapidly over a high heat. When nearly all evaporated, add the stock and reduce rapidly to one-quarter of the original volume until you have a nicely thickened sauce.

3___Add the cassis, half the blackcurrants and the butter and whisk well. Taste and adjust the seasoning, then strain through a fine sieve into a clean saucepan.

4___Add the rest of the blackcurrants and stir well, being careful not to break them up.

TO SERVE

1___Slice the rested loins and drain well on kitchen paper.

2___Arrange the warmed cooked leeks on warm plates and top with the sliced loin. Spoon over the sauce including a few whole blackcurrants.

Venison Chorizo with Dark Chocolate

MAKES 1KG
Preparation: 30 mins
Drying: 3–4 weeks

900g venison shoulder meat, completely free of gristle and sinew, chilled to a temperature of -2°C
28g curing salt (containing 0.6% sodium nitrite)
2g ground white pepper
20g smoked paprika
3g garlic powder
3g dextrose
2g sodium ascorbate
1g starter culture
100g dark chocolate drops
hog casings

This is an adaptation of another cured classic meat, this time Spanish chorizo. The dark chocolate twist works really well with this lovely spice mix, and with the venison of course.

1___Use a meat mincer fitted with an 8mm plate to mince the venison.
2___Put the minced venison into a large bowl, add all the dry ingredients and then the chocolate and mix together thoroughly with your hands.
3___Stuff the mixture into hog casings and twist into 15–20cm links or tie into rings.
4___Hang the sausages in a warm humid environment with a temperature of 24–26°C for 12–14 hours with very little airflow – in an airing cupboard with some damp towels is ideal. At this point, the sausages should feel quite firm and look redder in colour.
5___Then hang the sausages in an environment with a temperature of 12–14°C and a relative humidity of 76–78% with little airflow – a cellar or pantry would work well – until it is quite firm to the touch, when it is ready to eat. This will typically take about 3–4 weeks.

Venison Burgers

MAKES 1KG
Preparation: 20 mins, plus chilling
Cooking: 6–8 minutes

1kg venison flank or shoulder trimmings
10g cooking salt
salt and freshly ground black pepper

Everybody loves a burger, and this recipe uses up all the flanks and shoulder trimmings from a venison carcass and turns them into a premium product that everybody will love.

1___Use a meat mincer fitted with an 8mm plate to mince the venison. Put the minced meat into a large bowl, add the salt and mix together thoroughly with your hands.
2___Mince the meat again, this time using a 5mm plate, but as the meat comes out of the mincer, you need to catch it and lay it down on a sheet of clingfilm with all the strands running the same way.
3___Roll the clingfilm around the venison and keep rolling until it forms a tight, sausage-shaped roll. Refrigerate until completely chilled.
4___Using a sharp knife, cut the chilled roll into patties. Season the outside of them, then cook on a barbecue or in a griddle pan over a high heat for 3–4 minutes each side or until cooked through.

Venison Loaf with Onions, Smoked Pancetta & Hot Roasted Beets

SERVES 6–8
Preparation: 20 mins, plus cooling and chilling
Cooking: about 1 hour 10 mins

1 tablespoon vegetable oil
300g smoked pancetta, cubed
3 onions, finely chopped
2 garlic cloves, finely chopped
500g minced venison
200g good-quality sausage meat
200g minced pheasant, duck or partridge
2 teaspoons dried oregano
1 teaspoon ground cinnamon
1 teaspoon ground allspice
1 teaspoon dried chilli flakes
3 slices of white bread, crusts removed, made into breadcrumbs
1 medium egg, beaten
4 tablespoons roughly chopped fresh parsley
freshly ground black pepper

cont'd

I've always liked meatloaf of any description, especially the American version that comes with gravy and collard greens. This recipe is especially delicious because it incorporates various meats and is topped with a smoky pancetta. The roasted coloured beets are an ideal accompaniment once mixed with the sherry vinegar and mustard dressing. If you can get hold of some African game, wildebeest, kudu or even zebra meat would be perfect in this dish.

1__Preheat the oven to 180°C/Gas 4.

2__Heat the oil in a frying pan, add the pancetta and cook until the fat runs and the pancetta is nicely browned. Remove from the pan with a slotted spoon, draining well, and transfer to kitchen paper, then set aside to place on top of the meatloaf.

3__Add the onions and garlic to the pan and cook for 5 minutes to soften slightly and take on a little colour, then leave to cool.

4__Meanwhile, put all the meats, except the pancetta, into a large bowl and mix in the oregano, cinnamon, allspice and chilli flakes.

5__Add the breadcrumbs, egg and parsley, and mix really well. Season with pepper.

6__Add the cooled onions and garlic to the meat mixture and mix well again.

7__Spoon the mixture into a 900g non-stick loaf tin and flatten well. Top with the sautéed pancetta cubes.

8__Cover with a double layer of oiled foil and secure around the tin. Sit in a baking tray (to catch any fat that may ooze out) and bake for about 1 hour or until the juices run clear when a knife is inserted into the centre.

9__Carefully remove from the oven and leave to cool.

10__Once cool, place a piece of stiff cardboard, cut to fit the top of the loaf tin perfectly, on top of the foil, then balance a couple of food cans on top and chill in the fridge overnight.

11__Remove from the tin, slice and wrap in clean foil or clingfilm. Keep in the fridge until you are ready to serve. The meatloaf slices can be reheated in a microwave when you want.

SERVES 4

Preparation: 10 minutes

Cooking: 45–50 minutes

---

4 medium red beetroots

4 medium yellow beetroots

4 medium red-ringed
  beetroots

1 head of fresh garlic, sliced
  horizontally in half

DRESSING

3 tablespoons sherry vinegar

2 tablespoons Dijon mustard

5 tablespoons extra virgin
  olive oil

salt and freshly ground black
  pepper

4 tablespoons chopped fresh
  basil

ROASTED BEETS

1___Preheat the oven to 220°C/Gas 7.

2___Put the beets into a roasting tray with the garlic. Cover tightly with foil and bake for 45–50 minutes or until a knife passes through the beets with little resistance.

3___Remove the tray from the oven. At this point, wearing rubber gloves (I find this the easiest way by far), remove the foil and peel away the skin – it will rub off easily.

4___Remove the cooked garlic flesh from the halved bulb of cloves and roughly crush to a paste.

5___Cut the beets into thin wedges and put into a bowl.

6___In a separate bowl, whisk the vinegar, mustard and oil together, then add salt and pepper and the basil and pasted garlic and really mix well.

7___Add the dressing to the beets and toss together, then serve warm with the meatloaf, along with creamy mashed potatoes.

Cold-smoked Venison Haunch with Pickled Sweet & Sour Cherries

MAKES ABOUT 1KG
Smoking: 4½ hours
Drying: 4–6 weeks

About 1kg boneless haunch of
  venison, preferably topside
  or thick flank, free of sinew
  and gristle

DRY CURE
40g curing salt (containing
  1% sodium nitrite and 0.8%
  potassium nitrate)
4g Roschi Rustical spice mix

Curing and smoking is probably one of the most popular methods of preserving meat. Haunch of venison is the perfect candidate for this method and will sit perfectly on any charcuterie platter. I always use a single muscle from a large haunch that is completely free of sinew and gristle for this recipe. Preferably use the topside or thick flank muscle and from a reasonably sized haunch either would probably weigh around a kilo.

1___ Mix the curing salt and spice mix together thoroughly and apply half to your venison haunch.

2___ Put into a strong plastic container and refrigerate for a week, turning over after 3 days.

3___ Apply the second half of the cure mix to the venison and refrigerate for a further 2 weeks, again ensuring that it is turned every three days.

4___ Remove the venison from container and wash off with lukewarm water.

5___ Place the venison in a smoker. I usually dry the venison for 2½ hours at 23°C and then cold smoke for 2 hours at the same temperature.

6___ Hang the venison in an environment with a temperature of 12–14°C and a relative humidity of about 72–75 per cent with little airflow – a cellar or pantry would work well – until it is quite firm to the touch, when it is ready to eat. This will typically take about 4–6 weeks.

7___ Either vacuum pack or freeze the venison to prevent it from drying out any further.

PICKLED SWEET & SOUR CHERRIES

1___ Sterilise a preserving jar, if storing the cherries, by filling with boiling water and leaving for 5 minutes, then tipping out. Leave to cool.

2___ Wash the cherries well in plenty of cold water and dry thoroughly.

3___ Carefully stone the fruit.

4___ Place the vinegar, lemon juice, salt, spices and sugar in a stainless steel saucepan and heat over a medium heat until the sugar has dissolved.

5___ Place the cherries in the sterilised jar, or in a china jug if using the cherries in the shorter term.

6___ Pour the syrup over the fruit, then seal or cover with clingfilm and leave to cool.

7___ Store in the fridge, where they will keep for up to two months.

SERVES 6–8
Preparation: 15 minutes
Cooking: about 10 minutes,
plus cooling

500g fresh dark cherries
300ml cider vinegar
juice of 2 large lemons
½ tablespoon sea salt
10 cloves
½ cinnamon stick
½ teaspoon ground allspice
250g dark brown muscovado
  sugar

HARE

Europe has a pretty healthy hare population; they also thrive in countries such as Canada, America and New Zealand. Having said that, with the onset of increased intensive farming the hare could become a rarer species. Another threat is from illegal poaching; hare meat can command a high price and, in the current global downturn, it is species such as hare and deer that really suffer.

For me, the meat is an acquired taste but, as you will see, we have tried to think outside the box. Some of these recipes are rather unusual, but all work well.

Please note that, under the Hares Preservation Act 1892, it is illegal to sell hares or leverets in England and Wales between 1 March and 31 July. This does not apply to imported hares.

Hare Confit with Caramel Walnuts

MAKES ABOUT 1.5KG
Brining: 8–12 hours
Cooking: 4–5 hours

---

1 large hare, jointed (a good butcher will do this for you)
1kg duck or pork fat, melted

BRINE
1kg water
160g cooking salt
1 teaspoon black peppercorns
1teaspoon juniper berries, crushed

I love confit, especially duck, and I adore pork rillettes, which are cooked the same way, but I had never seen game confit anywhere, so I had a go with a hare. It worked and was absolutely delicious. It should keep in the fridge for a good month, but I suspect, when tasted, it won't last that long! It may sound odd serving caramel walnuts with it, but it really adds a sweet edge to the finished dish. A note of caution, however: because of the high temperatures reached by the sugar, you will need to keep a careful watch over all stages; this is not one to do unsupervised or with children!

HARE CONFIT

1___Mix together the ingredients for the brine and submerge the hare joints in it for 8–12 hours.

2___Preheat the oven to 100°C.

3___Remove the hare from the brine, place in a casserole dish and cover with your chosen fat. Place in the oven for 4–5 hours until the hare is fork tender. Remove and leave until the meat is cool enough to pull from the bones with your fingers.

4___Place the shredded meat in ramekins and cover with a layer of fat.

SERVES 4–6
Preparation: 20 mins
Cooking: 15 mins

250g caster sugar
8 tablespoons cold water
20 walnut halves

CARAMEL WALNUTS

1___Melt the sugar with the water in a small, heavy saucepan over a low heat, stirring gently until all the sugar crystals are dissolved. When this has happened, stop stirring and bring it to a rapid boil, then cook until the mixture turns a dark golden caramel colour. This will take about 10 minutes.

2___Turn off the heat but keep the caramel warm. Using two wooden skewers, pick up the walnut halves and dip them into the hot caramel sauce, coating them well. Transfer to a sheet of silicone paper and leave for the caramel to harden.

Hare & Venison Sausages
with Redcurrant & Juniper

MAKES 1KG
Preparation: 30 mins

500g boneless venison
   shoulder
300g boneless hare meat
150g dried breadcrumbs
   (made from bread that has
   been toasted)
15g cooking salt
2g ground white pepper
1g ground nutmeg
3g dried thyme
50ml iced water
1 heaped tablespoon
   redcurrant and juniper jelly
hog casings

Gamey and rich, these would make the ultimate sausage casserole.

1___Use a meat mincer fitted with a 5mm plate to mince the venison and hare meat.
2___Put the minced meat into a large bowl.
3___Mix the breadcrumbs, salt, spices and thyme together, then add to the minced meat and mix together thoroughly with your hands.
4___Add the iced water and mix thoroughly again.
5___Add the redcurrant and juniper jelly and mix well again.
6___Stuff the mixture into hog casings and twist into 10–15cm links.
7___Refrigerate until ready to use.

Hare Dumplings with Orzo Pasta & Parsley Broth

SERVES 4
Preparation: 35 mins
Cooking: 10 mins

plain flour, for dusting

about 750ml game stock (see page 214) or chicken stock

salt and freshly ground black pepper

100g cooked orzo pasta, or any other very small pasta

4 tablespoons chopped fresh parsley

DUMPLINGS

500g minced hare meat

50g salted butter, melted and cooled

75g chickpea (gram) flour or fine ground rice flour

1 small red onion, finely chopped

2 garlic cloves, chopped

½ teaspoon ground cumin

½ teaspoon ground coriander

½ teaspoon ground turmeric

2 tablespoons runny honey

4 tablespoons chopped fresh parsley

This really is a very simple recipe. For the dumplings, all you do is pulse the ingredients together in a food-processor, but no need to go mad – just enough to bring the mixture together. By poaching the meatballs in the stock, you get a very hearty, full-flavoured broth that is then bulked out with a little cooked pasta and finished with plenty of fresh parsley.

1___Put all the ingredients for the dumplings into a food-processor, seasoning with salt and pepper, and pulse until the mixture has just come together.

2___Using floured hands, roll the mixture into small dumplings the size of large cherry tomatoes.

3___Heat the stock in a large open pan. Check the seasoning and adjust if necessary.

4___Once the stock is simmering, drop in the dumplings, bring back to a simmer and cook for 8–10 minutes.

5___Add the cooked pasta to the stock, stir in and leave to warm through.

6___Serve the dumplings in warm deep bowls, adding enough stock to come halfway up the meatballs, sprinkled with the chopped parsley.

Braised Hare Faggots

SERVES 6–8
Preparation: 45 mins, plus cooling and chilling
Cooking: 1 hour

350g pork back fat

meat from 1 large hare, about 750g

300g lamb's liver

300g belly pork

450g lamb, pig or ox heart

100ml vegetable oil

4 onions, finely chopped

4 garlic cloves, crushed

½ teaspoon freshly grated nutmeg

½ teaspoon ground mace

2 tablespoons dried sage

8 tablespoons chopped fresh parsley

2 tablespoons chopped fresh tarragon

2 tablespoons dried thyme

4 medium eggs, beaten

6 tablespoons Worcestershire sauce

6 tablespoons dried breadcrumbs

salt and freshly ground black pepper

1 litre boiling well-flavoured brown chicken stock

The best faggots I ever had were in Swansea Market in Wales. They were soft and packed full of delicious flavour. Here is my version, which, while not traditional because I've added herbs, spices and garlic, does retain the essential authenticity by including heart, liver and back fat. I used to wrap mine in lamb caul fat, a thin lining from the inside of the animal, but it's becoming increasingly difficult to get hold of. If, however, you can source caul fat, then wrap each raw faggot in a thin layer before chilling. This recipe also works well with venison and wild goose. Having said that, some African game would also be ideal for faggots – try ostrich, warthog, springbok, kudu or wildebeest meat.

1___Use a mincer fitted with a 5mm plate to mince the fat, followed by all the meats.

2___Heat the vegetable oil in a large sauté pan, add the onions and garlic and cook for 10 minutes until slightly softened.

3___Add the spices and cook for a further 2 minutes, then leave to cool.

4___Transfer the cooled onion mixture to a bowl. Add the minced meat mixture and mix well, then add the herbs.

5___Next, add the eggs, Worcestershire sauce and the breadcrumbs, then season with salt and pepper.

6___Dust your hands with flour and shape into 100g balls, about the size of a small apple, then cover with clingfilm and chill for 15 minutes to firm up.

7___Preheat the oven to 190°C/Gas 5.

8___Pack the faggots nice and neatly into a deep roasting tray.

9___Spoon over the boiling chicken stock, which should just come three-quarters of the way up the faggots. Cover with foil and cook in the oven for about 40 minutes.

10__Remove the foil and cook for a further 20 minutes to reduce the sauce and allow the faggots to brown nicely.

11__Serve with the gravy, along with mushy peas and mashed potatoes.

Sautéed Hare Fillets
with Celeriac & Potato Gratin

SERVES 4
Preparation: 20 mins
Cooking: about 50 mins,
plus resting

350g peeled celeriac (500g
    unprepared weight)
350g potatoes, peeled
salt and freshly ground black
    pepper
600ml whipping cream
4 garlic cloves, crushed
50g unsalted butter
1 tablespoon oil
2 long back strap fillets of hare,
    secondary skin and sinew
    removed and then cut in half,
    making 4 fillets

This simple dish can be made the day before and then gently warmed in a moderate oven or in the microwave, which is brilliant for warming dishes like this. The purists may sneer, but I'm all for getting the best result possible with the least amount of fuss. Hare fillets need very little cooking – just minutes in fact – so take care not to overcook them. Remember to follow the usual rule with game and rest the hare for as long as you cooked it. Fillets of small African game are perfect alternatives. When I visited Africa all the game I ate worked well with British recipes, but the smaller were best when sautéing the loins. Try gemsbok, springbok or antelope, but ensure you undercook the meat, as these are lean beasts.

1___Preheat the oven to 190°C/Gas 5.

2___Cut the celeriac into quarters, and then cut into thin slices about 5mm thick.

3___Slice the potatoes in the same fashion, then rinse well in cold water.

4___Put both vegetables into a large saucepan, cover with cold water and add a couple of teaspoons of salt. Cover the pan, bring to the boil, then reduce the heat and simmer for 2 minutes – this helps to soften the vegetables and gives a much nicer end result. Drain well.

5___Carefully cover the base of a 24cm square baking dish, 5cm deep, with pieces of celeriac, overlapping them quite generously. Repeat with the potatoes. Season well with salt and pepper. Continue layering until all the celeriac and potato is used up.

6___Bring the cream and the garlic to the boil in a saucepan and then carefully pour over the celeriac and potato. Press down with a potato masher.

7___Bake in the oven for about 40 minutes – you may want to press down with the masher during the cooking period. The gratin should be well coloured and reduced, and a skewer or knife should penetrate the creamy cake with very little resistance. If you can make this the day before, all the better, then simply re-warm, covered, in a microwave or moderate oven.

8___When ready to eat, heat the butter with the oil in a frying pan until it starts to turn a nutty brown colour.

9___Season the hare fillets well with salt and pepper, add to the pan and sauté for 3–4 minutes on all sides. Do not overcook!

10___Remove the pan from the heat when the hare is still slightly undercooked, then transfer the fillets to a warm plate, cover loosely with foil and leave to rest in a warm place for 3–4 minutes.

11___Spoon the reheated creamy gratin into a warm deep bowl.

12___Slice the pink cooked hare fillets on a long angle, then pat with a piece of kitchen paper to remove any bloody juices and serve alongside the gratin.

Steamed Hare, Fat Bacon & Parsley Roll

**MAKES 2 X 15CM
ROLLS; SERVES 4–6**
**Preparation: 20 mins, plus
cooling**
Cooking: about 1 hour

This works well as a starter or as an accompaniment to a game main course such as roasted hare, wild goose or wild boar. A lot of people seem to think that suet pastry, either in its savoury or sweet form, is heavy and leaden, but adding egg and using self-raising flour makes it nice and light. Just remember to work quickly when rolling out the pastry, as the raising agents are activated when you add any liquid. This dish can also be cooked and then unwrapped and re-wrapped in clingfilm and reheated in a microwave on medium power. One last thing: serve with lots of game gravy and a little freshly made English mustard and extra redcurrant jelly.

FILLING

150g fat bacon, cut into 1cm
    pieces
1 small onion, finely chopped
2 tablespoons redcurrant jelly
2 tablespoons chopped fresh
    parsley
freshly ground black pepper
300g hare loin, secondary skin
    and sinew removed, cut into
    2cm pieces

PASTRY

225g self-raising flour
a pinch of salt
$\frac{1}{4}$ teaspoon cracked black
    pepper
6 heaped tablespoons chopped
    fresh parsley
115g shredded beef or lamb
    suet
1 medium egg, beaten, plus
    another for sealing
about 2 tablespoons cold water

FILLING

1___Heat a large frying pan, add the bacon and cook for about 10 minutes until nice and crisp. Remove the bacon from the pan with a slotted spoon, draining well, and transfer to kitchen paper. Add the onion to the pan and cook to get a nice colour, then add to the bacon. Leave to cool.

2___Spoon the cooled bacon and onion into a bowl and add the redcurrant jelly and parsley. Season well with pepper – no salt is needed – and mix in the raw hare.

PASTRY

1___Put the flour, salt, cracked pepper, parsley and suet into the bowl of an electric mixer fitted with a dough hook or paddle. Mix together on a slow speed.

2___Mix in the beaten egg and enough of the water to make a soft but not sticky dough.

ROLLS

1___Roll the dough out on a floured work surface to about 5mm thick and the size of a large A4 sheet of paper, give or take a few centimetres. Work the dough quickly, as the raising agents will be working away and the dough will start to rise.

2___Brush the outside edge really well with the beaten egg and then spread the hare and bacon mixture across the whole surface of the pastry evenly. Starting at one end, roll up loosely until fully rolled up with the other end on top, then cut in half. Fold the ends under and seal the edge of the top end well with beaten egg.

3___Place each roll on a well-buttered piece of foil 4–5cm larger than the roll and again roll up loosely, then twist the ends of the foil to make a fairly tight roll.

4___Pop the rolls into a steamer and steam for 40–45 minutes. The pastry will expand into the foil, making the rolls nice and tight.

5___Remove from the steamer and leave to cool for 10 minutes.

6___Unroll the rolls and slice thickly. Serve with game gravy (see page 217), English mustard and extra redcurrant jelly.

Pan-fried Hare Loin Fillets
with Baked Stuffed Chilli & Ginger Aubergines

SERVES 4
**Preparation: 35 mins, plus
cooling**
Cooking: just over 1 hour

4 tablespoons olive oil, plus
    another 4 tablespoons or so
    for cooking the aubergines
1 small red onion, finely
    chopped
4 garlic cloves, chopped
1 tablespoon finely chopped
    fresh red chilli
2 tablespoons peeled and very
    finely chopped fresh ginger
2 medium aubergines
salt and freshly ground black
    pepper
150ml mirin
2 tablespoons sherry vinegar
1 tablespoon sesame oil
50g unsalted butter
saddle loins from 2 hares,
    making 4 pieces, secondary
    skin and sinew removed

Hare meat can be quite strong, so combining it with big flavour profiles is not a problem. The soft texture of the baked aubergines, coupled with the chilli and ginger kick, works really well and fits perfectly with the simply cooked loins.

1___Preheat the oven to 220°C/Gas 7.

2___Heat 4 tablespoons olive oil in a saucepan, add the onion, garlic, chilli and ginger and cook over a high heat for about 8 minutes until the ingredients are well coloured. Remove the pan from the heat and leave to cool.

3___Heat the remaining 4 tablespoons olive oil in a large frying pan.

4___Using a sharp knife, slice the aubergines in half lengthways and score the inside three or four times. Season the aubergines well, then place two halves cut side down in the hot oil and cook for 4–5 minutes until well coloured. Turn over and cook for a further 3–4 minutes, remove from the pan and put into a baking dish.

5___Repeat the process with the other two aubergine halves – you may need to add a little more oil – then put the baking dish with the aubergines into the oven and cook for 20 minutes or until softened.

6___Meanwhile, put the mirin, vinegar and sesame oil into a saucepan, bring to the boil and cook down for about 5–8 minutes until thick and syrupy.

7___Once the aubergines are ready, remove the baking dish from the oven.Spoon over the cooked onions and ginger, mix evenly and then season well.

8___Spoon over the thick mirin glaze and return to the oven for a further 20 minutes or until well coloured, cooked and nicely glazed. The aroma will be amazing.

9___While the aubergines are finishing, cook the hare fillets. Heat the butter in a frying pan until foaming and slightly browned. Season the hare loins well , add to the hot butter and cook for 2–3 minutes. Turn the loins over and brown again for a couple of minutes, ensuring that the meat is still nice and rare.

10_Transfer the loins to a warm plate, cover loosely with foil and leave to rest in a warm place for at least 5 minutes.

TO SERVE

1___When the aubergines are ready, remove from the oven and leave to cool slightly.

2___Carefully lift the aubergines onto warm serving plates or bowls. You may need two spatulas for this.

3___Slice each hare loin into two or three very long shards, arrange on top of the aubergine and serve.

Hare & White Chocolate Salami

MAKES 1KG
Preparation: 30 mins
Drying: 3–4 weeks

900g boneless hare meat, completely free of gristle and sinew, chilled to a temperature of -2°C
28g curing salt (containing 0.6% sodium nitrite)
2g ground white pepper
3g dextrose
2g sodium ascorbate
1g starter culture
100g white chocolate drops
hog casings

Yes, I know this sounds odd, but with hare being a fairly strong-flavoured meat, the addition of sweet white chocolate absolutely complements it. This was definitely one of my better ideas.

1__Use a meat mincer fitted with an 8mm plate to mince the hare.
2__Put the minced hare into a large bowl, add all the dry ingredients and then the chocolate and mix together thoroughly with your hands.
3__Stuff the mixture into hog casings and twist into 15–20cm links or tie into rings.
4__Hang the sausages in a warm humid environment with a temperature of 24–26°C for 12–14 hours with very little airflow – in an airing cupboard with some damp towels is ideal. At this point, the sausages should feel quite firm and look redder in colour.
5__Then hang the sausages in an environment with a temperature of 12–14°C and a relative humidity of 76–78% with little airflow – a cellar or pantry would work well – until it is quite firm to the touch, when it is ready to eat. This will typically take about 3–4 weeks.

RABBIT

Drive, or for that matter walk, along most roads and the chances are you will see a rabbit or two in or near a verge. I'm not just talking about open countryside; roundabouts, central reservations on dual carriageways and even outside retail parks. Rabbits are everywhere, but their origin is up for many a discussion. I go with the Romans introducing them to Britain and then the Normans almost domesticating them. The rest is history as they say. I'm not really sure why we do not eat more of an animal that is commonplace and also a pest. The meat is delicious, cheap and can be cooked very easily. I suppose, as with deer, the fact that an adorable cartoon has been made about them (*Watership Down*), you are really up against it from the word go. If you can look beyond that, there are a number of recipes here for you to try. I would urge you to buy wild rabbit, the younger the better, as opposed to farmed, which mostly comes from China.

Sous Vide Rabbit

SERVES
Preparation: 10 mins
Cooking: 3 hours

4 rabbit hind legs, back bone removed (a good butcher will do this for you)
vacuum pouch for sous vide cooking
knob of unsalted butter
small sprig of fresh thyme
salt and freshly ground black pepper

Sous vide, which is becoming an increasingly popular method of cooking, is a good way to deal with rabbit, especially the hind legs used in this dish.

1___Place the rabbit legs in the pouch with the other ingredients and vacuum seal.

2___Place in a water bath at 78°C for 3 hours.

3___Remove and place in iced water to chill through, then store in fridge until ready to use.

Buttermilk-marinated Fried Rabbit

SERVES 4–6
Preparation: 15 mins, plus marinating
Cooking: about 20 mins

1 small rabbit, secondary skin and sinew removed, washed well and dried with kitchen paper
500ml buttermilk
1 teaspoon ground turmeric
½ teaspoon salt
½ teaspoon ground black pepper
1 tablespoon runny honey
about 350g self-raising flour
lard, oil, dripping or animal fat, for deep-frying

For this dish you really need a young rabbit; as they get older, they tend to be better for braising or stewing. Buttermilk has long been used for marinating meat in order to tenderise it. Indian and Bangladeshi cooks use yogurt with great success, which works on roughly the same principle. Classic fried chicken in American cooking features buttermilk both for softening the flesh and to add flavour. I recommend that you leave the rabbit to marinate for at least 24 hours, but I have left it for as long as three days with good results. When it comes to frying I tend to use lard, as they do in the US, because it gives a crisper result and with a good, clean flavour, but any oil or animal fat will do. Another good tip is to fry the rabbit three or four pieces at a time, then salt and leave to rest in a warm place for a few minutes.

1 Place the rabbit side down on a chopping board. Using a sharp knife, cut the flesh away from the inside of one back leg. Pull the leg away from the carcass and then back on itself so that the ball and socket joint pops open. Cut away the last part of the leg and remove completely. Repeat with the other leg.

2 Next, cut the saddle out, roughly three-quarters of the way along the back of the rabbit, slicing and chopping right through. Then cut the saddle into three pieces.

3 Lastly, pull the front leg away from the rib cage and slice straight through, keeping as close to the body as possible. The front leg of a rabbit, unlike the rear leg, has no ball and socket joint, so it will slice through easily. Repeat with the other front leg and leave them both whole.

4 Put the buttermilk, turmeric, salt, pepper and honey into a bowl and whisk well. Add the rabbit pieces and really coat well in the buttermilk mixture. Cover the bowl tightly with clingfilm so that all air is excluded and leave to marinate in the fridge for a minimum of 24 hours.

5 When ready to cook, heat whatever cooking medium you want for your rabbit in a deep-fat fryer or deep saucepan to 185°C.

6 Lift all the pieces of rabbit out of the bowl, scraping off most of the buttermilk mixture, then place in another bowl containing the flour. Really coat the rabbit well, ensuring that all the small crevices of the meat are dusted with flour.

7 Fry in the hot oil in small batches for 4–5 minutes, then flip over and cook for a further 2–3 minutes.

8 Remove from the oil, place on kitchen paper and season lightly with salt and pepper. Leave to rest in a warm place for 5 minutes, then tuck in! Real finger food.

Wild Rabbit Paella

**SERVES 4 AS A MAIN;
8 AS A STARTER**
**Preparation: 20 mins
Cooking: about 40 mins,
plus standing**

6 tablespoons olive oil, plus
  extra if needed
2 small onions, finely chopped
3 garlic cloves, chopped
1 red pepper, deseeded and cut
  into 1cm pieces
½ teaspoon smoked paprika
a pinch or two of saffron
  threads
2 tablespoons tomato purée
350g paella rice
1 small rabbit, chopped into 12
  pieces: legs into 2, saddle into
  4, shoulders into 4
125g raw prawns in their shells
125g prepared baby squid
about 600ml boiling fish or
  chicken stock
salt and freshly ground black
  pepper
125g live mussels
125g shucked baby scallops
1 large bunch fresh parsley,
  roughly chopped

I once had this dish over a lazy Sunday lunchtime in Spain some years ago with the family. In fact, it was so good I asked the chef for the recipe, and here it is. It has such a depth of flavour, and the colour is amazing.

1___Preheat the oven to 200°C/Gas 6.

2___Heat the oil in a paella pan or ovenproof sauté pan with a tight-fitting lid, add the onions, garlic and red pepper and cook for about 10 minutes until the pepper releases its colour slightly.

3___Add the paprika, saffron and tomato purée, and mix well.

4___Next, add the rice and stir to coat well in the oil and onion mixture.

5___Then add the rabbit pieces and mix really well.

6___Add the prawns and squid, and mix well again.

7___Pour in the boiling stock and add just a little salt and some pepper, then mix well.

8___Bring back to the boil, then cover with the lid, transfer the pan to the oven and cook for 12–14 minutes.

9___Stir the mussels and scallops into the pan, re-cover and return to the oven for a further 8–10 minutes.

10__Remove the pan from the oven and stir well – you may need to add a little more oil.

11__Re-cover and leave to stand for 10 minutes, then serve with the chopped parsley.

Wild Rabbit with Olive Oil, Sage & Artichokes

SERVES 2-3
Preparation: 20 mins, plus cooling and chilling
Cooking: 1 hour 30 mins

1 wild rabbit, cleaned well

2 carrots, peeled

1 large onion

2 garlic cloves

2 celery sticks

8 fresh sage leaves, roughly chopped

1 sprig of fresh thyme

2 bay leaves

1 medium glass dry white wine

385g jar artichokes in oil, drained well

salt and freshly ground black pepper

200–300ml extra virgin olive oil – enough to cover the cooked rabbit and artichokes completely

I had this dish in Italy once, and it was so simple and tasty that it blew me away. A large tureen was passed round the restaurant and you helped yourselves as a middle course. The cooked meat and vegetables, flavoured with fresh sage and artichokes, make an utterly unique dish; I've never had anything like it. Eat it at room temperature with crusty bread.

1__Cut the rabbit in half and place in a saucepan.

2__Chop up all the vegetables and add to the rabbit along with herbs and the wine.

3__Cover with cold water and bring to a simmer, topping up the water as needed. Cook gently for 1 hour 30 minutes or until the rabbit is very tender, but do not overcook.

4__Leave to cool for 15 minutes, then lift the rabbit from the cooking liquor, gently pull off all the meat in large chunks and put into a bowl.

5__Strain the stock off but reserve all the cooked vegetables.

6__Roughly chop the artichokes, add the sage and mix well.

7__Add the artichoke mixture to the cooked rabbit meat and mix well again.

8__Add all the strained vegetables and mix well. Season well with salt and pepper.

9__While still warm, cover the whole mixture with olive oil.

10_Cover the bowl with clingfilm and leave to cool completely, then refrigerate for 48 hours.

11_Remove from the fridge 1 hour before eating and served spooned into bowls with crusty bread.

Roasted Saddle of Rabbit with New Potatoes, Broad Beans & Mint Hollandaise

SERVES 4
Preparation: 25 mins
Cooking: about 15 mins, plus resting; about 15 mins for the hollandaise

MINT HOLLANDAISE

100ml white wine
50ml white wine vinegar
50ml water
1 small celery stick
2 medium shallots, thinly sliced
1 teaspoon white peppercorns, crushed
5–6 fresh mint stalks, chopped
4 medium egg yolks, at room temperature
150g unsalted butter, melted and warm
squeeze of lemon juice
salt
15 fresh mint leaves, finely chopped

cont'd

A very simple recipe, but like all dishes that are simple it relies on great-quality ingredients. Young rabbit is so delicious and so very lean that it needs careful attention when roasting quickly. This is why I lightly dust it with starch to seal in the juices as much as possible. The first new potatoes, lightly boiled with fresh mint sprigs and salt, are all you need to accompany it – and, of course, broad beans, one of my favourites just lightly boiled. I sometimes use frozen broad beans, as they are superb quality; likewise frozen peas. Later in the year, runner or French beans are also excellent. A lot of people get worried about making hollandaise, and I can understand why. It's a tricky sauce to perfect, but follow a few basic rules and you won't fail. I adore hollandaise of any flavour with new potatoes; it's a great combination.

HOLLANDAISE

1___Make this while preheating the oven for the rabbit to 220°C/Gas 7.

2___Put the wine, vinegar, water, celery, shallots, peppercorns and mint stalks into a small saucepan. Bring to the boil and then simmer gently until you have roughly half the original quantity left, so about 100ml once strained.

3___Pop the egg yolks into a glass or metal bowl set over a saucepan of gently simmering water and whisk to break up. Be careful not to cook the yolks at this point.

4___Straightaway, reheat the reduction until simmering, then slowly pour onto the yolks, whisking quickly.

5___The yolks will start to foam up considerably, but ensure that you keep the edges of the bowl clean with the whisk. The secret is to keep whisking as the mixture thickens (this is the protein coagulating) – I take the bowl on and off the simmering pan to achieve a fine, thick foam and to avoid scrambling the eggs. Don't rush the process; it may take a few minutes. If the mixture is not cooked through and thick, the butter will not hold itself and will curdle and split.

6___Once thick and very creamy (there will be steam rising from a whisk full of egg), remove the bowl from the pan of water.

7___Gradually add the warm melted butter, whisking all the time – the sauce will thicken again and hold the weight of the butter.

8___Once all the butter is incorporated, add the lemon juice, a little salt and the chopped mint leaves. You may also need to add a dash of hot water to let the mixture down to a nice pouring consistency.

9___Pour into a jug or bowl, cover with clingfilm and keep warm, but not hot or the sauce will split. I find a Thermos flask perfect for this purpose.

RABBIT AND VEGETABLES

500g new potatoes, sliced
  lengthways
salt and freshly ground black
  pepper
2 sprigs of fresh mint
50g unsalted butter
2 tablespoons any oil
4 saddles of rabbit, the silver
  skin (sinew) on the top of the
  saddle removed with a sharp
  knife
2 tablespoons cornflour,
  arrowroot or any other
  starch, such as potato or
  tapioca flour
350g cooked skinned broad
  beans, the smaller the better,
  cooked and warm
3 tablespoons extra virgin
  olive oil

RABBIT AND VEGETABLES

1___Place the potatoes in a saucepan of water on the stove, add a little salt and the mint sprigs and bring to the boil. Reduce the heat and simmer for about 15 minutes until cooked.

2___While the potatoes are simmering, heat the butter with the oil in a small ovenproof frying pan until bubbling and light brown.

3___Dust the saddles with the starch and season well with salt and pepper, then place top side down in the hot butter mixture and cook for 2–3 minutes to seal the starch.

4___Turn the saddles over, then transfer the pan to the oven and cook for 7–8 minutes.

5___Turn the saddles back again and return to the oven for a further 4 minutes.

6___Remove the pan from the oven, then transfer the saddles to a warm plate, cover loosely with foil and leave to rest in a warm place for 10 minutes.

7___Meanwhile, drain the potatoes well and return to the pan. Add the cooked broad beans and the extra virgin olive oil and mix well, then add a touch of seasoning.

8___When the saddles have rested, transfer to a chopping board. Using a sharp knife, slice down each side of the backbone of one saddle and carve off the loins. They should still be pink on the inside. Turn over and carve off the small fillets. Cover with foil and keep warm while you repeat with the other three saddles.

TO SERVE

1___To serve, slice each of the loins into two long shards and overlap on a warm plate, two loins each plus fillets.

2___Place the potatoes and broad beans next to the rabbit.

3___Finally, re-whisk the hollandaise (as it will have set slightly) and spoon over the warm rabbit. That's it – simple but delicious.

Rabbit & Potato Pie

SERVES 6–8
Preparation: 20 mins
Cooking: 1 hour 15 mins

85g unsalted butter

1 medium onion, finely
   chopped

350g shortcrust pastry

plain flour, for dusting

750g potatoes, boiled in their
   skins until cooked through,
   then thinly sliced (don't
   worry if the potatoes break
   up slightly)

salt and freshly ground black
   pepper

200g rabbit meat from the
   legs or saddle, cut into 5mm
   pieces

1 medium egg, beaten

My late grandmother used to bake these for me in old Fray Bentos tins, to keep me sustained while thumbing back to the Lake District from Blackpool in the early 1980s. In Lancashire they are known as 'whistlers', which harks back to the war years when meat was scarce. Meat and potato pies, a great Lancastrian tradition, suddenly had to be made with little or no meat at all, and so if you were fortunate enough to come across a piece of meat in your pie, you would whistle. As the war went on, my mother said there wasn't a lot of whistling at the dinner table. Here I've added a little rabbit, a perfect match in my eyes.

1___Preheat the oven to 180°C/Gas 4.

2___Heat 25g of the butter in a frying pan, add the onion and cook gently for about 6–8 minutes until soft, but don't allow it to colour.

3___Thinly roll out two-thirds of the pastry on a lightly floured work surface and use to line a 24cm round, 3.5cm deep, loose-bottomed flan tin. Trim the edges with a knife or pair of scissors, leaving a 2cm overhang.

4___Lay half the potatoes in the base of the pastry case and season with salt and pepper. Melt the remaining butter, then pour over the potatoes and scatter over half the rabbit pieces and half the onion. Repeat the process, starting with the potatoes, leaving the contents standing proud of the pastry case.

5___Thinly roll out the final one-third of the pastry. Brush the top edge of the pastry case with the egg and lay the remaining rolled-out pastry over the top. Seal well, thumb up the edge and flute or crimp to decorate, then brush the pastry all over with the remaining egg.

6___Put the pie on a baking tray, pop in the oven and bake for 1 hour or until nicely browned. Remove from the oven and leave to cool for at least 30 minutes.

7___To serve, slice and eat warm or cold with pickle.

Simple Rabbit & Green Peppercorn Pâté

SERVES 6–8
**Preparation: 35–40 mins,
plus marinating, cooling
and chilling**
**Cooking: about 1 hour 15
mins**

1 medium rabbit

400g pork back fat

1 medium pork fillet, sinew
  removed but any fat is fine to
  keep

100ml brandy

100ml port

4 shallots, chopped

2 garlic cloves, crushed

salt and freshly ground black
  pepper

50g green peppercorns in
  brine, rinsed well and
  drained

I have been cooking this terrine for many years. Not only is it tasty but also very easy to make. If you want to be very precise, you can pass the mixture through a fine sieve to achieve a very fine texture, but it's not necessary. When processing the mixture, take care not to do so for too long, otherwise the friction can heat up the raw mixture, cooking it slightly. Pressing the pâté while chilling makes it easier to slice, but also ensures that it is nice and dense.

1___Carefully remove all the meat from the rabbit. Remove the silver skin (sinew) from the loins and discard, and also any small tendons. If you find the kidneys and liver, then all the better – add them to the rabbit meat in a bowl.

2___Chop the back fat up into small pieces and add to the rabbit.

3___Chop the pork fillet into chunks and also add to the rabbit.

4___Pour over the booze and add the shallots, garlic and a good seasoning of salt and pepper. Mix well. Cover with clingfilm and leave in the fridge for 24 hours, stirring occasionally.

5___Preheat the oven to 190°C/Gas 5.

6___Use a meat mincer fitted with a 5mm plate to mince all the ingredients and keep cold.

7___Whizz in a food-processor to a smooth paste, but don't overprocess. Spoon into a bowl and mix with a wooden spoon or spatula. At this point, if you want to be really cheffy, you can pass the mixture through a fine sieve; it depends on the texture you prefer.

8___Beat in the peppercorns and re-season well with salt and pepper.

9___Spoon the mixture into a 10 x 25 x 8cm terrine dish or suitable baking dish and press down well. Cover tightly with foil and sit in a deep baking tray. Boil a kettleful of water and pour boiling water into the tray until it comes halfway up the sides of the dish. Carefully transfer the tray to the oven and cook for 1 hour 15 minutes.

10_To check if the pâté is cooked, unwrap and insert a skewer – the juices should run clear. Carefully remove the tray from the oven, lift out the dish and then stand on a clean tray. Leave the pâté to cool, then top with a piece of stiff cardboard, cut to fit the top of the terrine perfectly. Place a couple of food cans on top and chill in the fridge overnight.

11_When ready to eat, remove the cans and card, place the dish in a deep bowl and pour in hot water from the tap so that it reaches 2cm from the top of the dish. Leave for 5 minutes, then lift out and turn upside down – the pâté should slide out easily. Slice and serve.

Andouille Bunny Burgers

MAKES 1KG
Preparation: 15 mins
Cooking: 10 mins

750g boneless rabbit meat (a
    good-sized wild rabbit would
    probably yield this amount)
250g boneless belly pork, cut
    into 2.5cm cubes
15g cooking salt
4g coarsely ground black
    pepper
2g dried thyme
2g garlic powder
2g chilli powder
2g smoked paprika

This is a fantastic way of using up rabbit as a change from the traditional rabbit stew and also a great way to get kids to try game. The addition of some belly pork provides much-needed fat for this very lean meat.

1   Use a meat mincer fitted with a 5mm plate to mince the rabbit and pork.

2   Put the minced meat into a large bowl, add all the remaining ingredients and mix together thoroughly with your hands until it starts to stick to them – this ensures adequate binding.

3   Form the meat mixture into about 10 patties, either by hand or using a burger press.

4   Cover with clingfilm and chill for a couple of hours before cooking.

5   For best results, cook on a charcoal barbecue over a high heat, or you can use a griddle pan, for about 5 minutes on each side or until cooked through.

Grey Squirrel Braised with Corn & Broad Beans

SERVES 4
Preparation: 25 mins, plus soaking
Cooking: about 1 hour 30 mins

BRAISE

½ teaspoon salt

¼ teaspoon freshly ground black pepper

565ml milk

2 small grey squirrels, skinned, cleaned and cut into quarters

4 tablespoons any oil

1 red pepper, deseeded and cut into 2cm pieces

1 large onion, cut into 2cm pieces

6 garlic cloves, crushed

2 celery sticks, cut into 2cm pieces

2 small carrots, peeled and cut into 2cm pieces

2 tablespoons tomato purée

about 750ml game stock (see page 214) or chicken stock

1 tablespoon cornflour, arrowroot or tapioca flour, mixed with 3–4 tablespoons cold water

CORN AND BEANS

2 tablespoons any oil

200g sweetcorn kernels cut from fresh corn on the cob

150g frozen baby broad beans, defrosted and patted dry with kitchen paper

When I sat down with my publisher, Kyle Cathie, I told her I wanted to write a book that was modern not only in its approach to preparing and cooking but also in the types of game it featured. It will take time for these new meats to be accepted, especially when you consider how long it has taken the British to get used to the idea of eating deer. Grey squirrel, another very nice meat, will divide us pretty neatly into two camps: the 'for' and 'against'. I find it difficult to understand the logic behind not eating them. We eat young chickens and baby lambs; grey squirrels are no different. Plus it's a non-native pest, that causes damage to woodland and threatens other wildlife – not least our native red squirrel. My only word of caution – use younger specimens; older ones can be tough, chewy and dry.

BRAISE

1___The day before, mix the salt and pepper into the milk in a large bowl, then add the squirrel pieces and coat well. Cover the bowl with clingfilm and leave in the fridge overnight or for a minimum of 12 hours.

2___The next day, drain the soaked squirrel, rinse in cold water and drain again.

3___Heat the oil in a deep saucepan, add the red pepper and onion and cook for about 10 minutes until they take on a good colour.

4___Next, add the garlic, celery and carrots and mix well, then stir in the tomato purée.
___Pop in the squirrel pieces and cover well with the stock.

5___Bring to the boil, then reduce the heat and gently simmer, uncovered, for about 1 hour 15 minutes. The cooking time will depend on the age of the animal, so check to see if the meat is tender and cooked through.

6___When the meat is ready, reduce the heat to very low.

CORN AND BEANS

1___Heat the oil in a large frying pan or wok, add the sweetcorn kernels and sauté over a high heat for about 2–3 minutes until they are nicely browned. They will 'pop' like popcorn, so you may need to place a piece of foil loosely over the pan.

2___Add the defrosted broad beans and warm through.

TO FINISH

1___Stir the starch mixture into the braise, bring back to a gentle simmer and cook just until the braise thickens nicely.

2___Add the sweetcorn and broad beans to the braise and stir in well, then serve.

WILD BOAR

Wild boar populate most of Europe and I have travelled to many countries that prize the meat very highly indeed. In Italy for instance, Sienna is famed for its boar, with shops selling entirely wild boar products from salami to preserved meat in fat. In the UK we have wild boar, but these are descended from escapees. Gloucestershire has an increasing wild population and they are starting to become a bit of a pest. My friend Peter Gott farms wild boar in Cumbria and has experimented with crossing with other breeds to get what he calls an Iron Age pig – a lighter, leaner pig that produces a very good end result. The meat is darker than normal pork and does have a gamey flavour. It roasts perfectly. Wild boar make great bacon, salami and even ham.

Wild Boar Kassler

MAKES 1KG
Preparation: 20 mins
Smoking: 20 mins

1kg boneless loin of wild boar

BRINE
1 litre chilled water
100g curing salt (containing 0.6% sodium nitrite)
3g dextrose
2g sodium ascorbate

I love this with fried potatoes, fried onions and a nice cold beer. Enough said.

1___Mix the cold water and salt together thoroughly in a large, deep strong plastic or stainless steel bowl or container until the salt has dissolved, then add the dextrose and sodium ascorbate.

2___Put the wild boar into the brine, ensuring that it is fully immersed, and leave in the fridge for 1 week.

3___Remove the meat from the brine and dry thoroughly. I usually do this in my smoker at a temperature of 60°C for about an hour.

4___Then apply a light smoke at 65°C for about 20 minutes.

5___Transfer the meat to a steam oven and steam at 78°C until a core temperature of 68°C is reached. Your wild boar is now ready to eat.

Braised Rice with Wild Boar Gravy

SERVES 4–6
Preparation: 20 mins
Cooking: 45–55 mins

I had a version of this many years ago for lunch in San Antonio, Texas. Sometimes us chefs think too much about food – we play around when there is really no need to and we should just keep it simple and straight to the point, as in this example. Here, the gravy moistens the fluffy braised rice and gives it a nice flavour. Almost any soft green vegetable will work in the rice, as it only needs a few minutes in the oven. I tasted warthog when I filmed in Nambia last year and it would work perfectly here in place of the boar.

GRAVY

1 tablespoon vegetable oil

3 teaspoons ground cumin

2 teaspoons ground cinnamon

1 tablespoon smoked paprika

2 teaspoon ground cinnamon

1 teaspoon dried chilli flakes

2 large onions, finely chopped

6 garlic cloves, chopped

500g minced boar or warthog
 – best from the shoulder and
 belly, about 20% fat

3 teaspoons dried oregano

400g can chopped tomatoes
 in juice

about 300ml water

2 tablespoons tomato purée

2 teaspoons sugar

salt and freshly ground black
 pepper

400g can pinto beans, drained

RICE

200g basmati rice, washed 3
 times in a sieve, then soaked
 in warm water for 10 minutes

100g wild rice, soaked
 overnight

2–3 tablespoons olive oil

50g baby leaf spinach, washed
 really well and drained well

about 350ml strong game
 stock (see page 214) or
 chicken stock

50g butter

GRAVY

1   Heat the vegetable oil in a saucepan, add all the spices and cook for 1 minute over a low heat – do not burn.

2   Add the onions and garlic and cook gently for about 10 minutes until the onions are softened.

3   Add the mince and break up well with a wooden spoon. Then cook for a few minutes, stirring well, until all the moisture has evaporated and the meat is starting to brown well.

4   Next, add the oregano, tomatoes, water, tomato purée and sugar, and bring up to a simmer. Mix well and taste and adjust the seasoning if necessary.

5   Finally, stir in the drained beans and cook gently, uncovered, for 30–40 minutes, stirring occasionally.

RICE

1   Preheat the oven to 200°C/Gas 6.

2   Drain both rices and rinse really well in a fine colander, then drain well.

3   Heat the olive oil in an ovenproof sauté pan, add the spinach and cook for a minute or two until wilted.

4   Add the drained rices and stir well, then add enough stock to come about 1cm above the rice.

5   Bring to the boil, season with salt and pepper and stir well.

6   Cover the pan, transfer to the oven and cook for 14–16 minutes until the rice is tender.

7   Remove the pan from the oven, add the butter and break the rice up with a fork. It should have a lovely aroma.

TO SERVE

Serve the rice into warm deep bowls and spoon over the boar gravy.

Grilled Wild Boar Rib-eyes
with Sweet–Sour & Bitter Chocolate Onions

SERVES 4
Preparation: 15 mins
Cooking: 40 mins

any oil, for cooking
8 small wild boar or warthog
   rib-eye steaks
salt and freshly ground black
   pepper

SAUCE
3 tablespoons olive oil
2 large onions, finely sliced
10g good-quality chicken stock
   cube, crumbled
150ml water
300ml red wine
a pinch of dried chilli flakes
2 tablespoons dark brown
   sugar
2 tablespoons sherry vinegar
30g bitter chocolate, chopped
freshly ground black pepper
   (probably no salt needed due
   to the stock cube, but check)

My good friend Peter Gott introduced me to this cut from his wild boar some years ago and I love it. The steaks are quite small, so two each is a must; the ratio of soft, creamy fat to flesh is ideal. These onions are a perfect foil for the richness of the meat, and while it sounds a bit weird, it really does work extremely well. Warthog would also be ideal for this recipe, as would blue wildebeest, or even kudu. I tend to use my barbecue all year round – including for cooking the Christmas turkey! So for me there is only one way to cook any steak, and that's on the barbecue grill, even in the rain.

ONIONS
1___Heat the olive oil in a large sauté pan, add the sliced onions and cook over a high heat for a couple of minutes to get some heat into them.
2___Add the stock cube and water, then reduce the heat, cover well and simmer for 20 minutes.
3___Stir in the wine, chilli flakes, sugar, vinegar, chocolate and pepper, then cook, uncovered, for about 15 minutes until you have a thickish sauce, but take care, as it may burn.

STEAKS
1___Heat the barbecue to medium. Meanwhile, clean the bars of the barbecue grill and oil lightly, then lightly oil the rib-eyes – oiling both stops the meat from sticking. Alternatively, if cooking on the stove, heat a large frying pan over a high heat and add a couple of tablespoons of oil.
2___Season the steaks well with salt and pepper and cook for 3–4 minutes on each side, getting as much colour on them as possible.
3___Remove from the grill or pan to a warm platter, loosely cover with foil and leave to rest in a warm place for the same amount of time you have grilled or fried them.
4___To serve, place the steaks on warm plates and serve the onions to one side. A little mash or some roasted potatoes is all you need to go with them.

Slow-roasted Rolled Wild Boar Belly
with Prunes, Harissa, Coriander & Pine Nuts

SERVES 6–8
Preparation: 20 mins
Cooking: about 3 hours 15
mins, plus resting

2kg piece of wild boar belly,
   boned but skin on
salt and freshly ground black
   pepper
50g pine nuts, toasted
25g fresh coriander
2–3 tablespoons harissa paste
125g pitted semi-dried prunes

This deceptively simple recipe is so delicious, I really can't add anything else to it to improve it. The rich meat and fat on a boar's belly needs some big flavours to cut the richness, and these few ingredients are a perfect foil. I use flavours like harissa very carefully, as it's so pungent, but here combined with the sweetness of the prunes and texture of the pine nuts it's ideal.

1___Preheat the oven to 160°C/Gas 3.

2___Lay the boar belly skin side down on a chopping board. Using a sharp knife, cut through the belly horizontally from the short side until you get to about 5cm from the other end. Do not slice right through.

3___Open up the belly so that you now have a large piece attached at one side like an open envelope.Season both sides well with salt and pepper, and then rub the harissa paste over right to the edges.

4___Next, lay the coriander across the meat, stalks and all, nice and evenly.

5___Finally, sprinkle over the pine nuts and prunes evenly.

6___Lay the flap back over the filling and roll up, from the long side, ensuring that you keep as much filling inside as you can. Using kitchen string tie well , but not too tightly, at regular intervals, starting from the middle, then both ends, and then finally filling in the gaps. This helps to stop the filling from falling out.

7___Place the roll on a baking tray and season really well. Pop in the oven and slow roast for 3 hours. Once cooked, the meat will be beautifully tender, easily pierced with a knife or skewer.

8___Remove the tray from the oven and tip off the delicious juices. These can be used as a base for a gravy or chilled and the fat used to sauté eggs or other meats.

9___Leave the meat to rest in a warm place for 15 minutes.

10__Turn the oven up to 200°C/Gas 6.

11__Carefully cut off the strings and discard. Using a long, sharp knife, cut the skin away from the soft, succulent fat, keeping as close as possible to the skin. It will come off in a large coiled sheet. Wrap the joint in foil and leave to rest in a warm place for a further 30–40 minutes.

12__Meanwhile, return the skin to the hotter oven and cook for about 12–15 minutes until crispy, turning occasionally, then remove from the oven, leave to cool and chop up.

13__When ready to serve, unwrap the cooked loin, slice thickly and serve with a big chunk of crispy skin. All you really need with this is some steamed broccoli or cauliflower, rolled through the cooking juices.

Hunter's Potato Bake

SERVES 4–6
Preparation: 20 mins
Cooking: about 1 hour 30 mins, plus cooling

6 tablespoons any oil

4 small onions, sliced 2–3mm thick, the same as the potatoes

1 tablespoon fresh thyme fronds

500g coarsely minced boar or very finely chopped belly or shoulder

10 medium waxy potatoes, peeled and sliced 2–3mm thick

2 tablespoons Worcestershire sauce

about 750ml boiling game stock (see page 214) or game gravy (see page 217)

salt and freshly ground black pepper

This can either be a stand-alone dish or take part in a game feast. I sometimes serve it with a fried pheasant or duck egg on top. A small amount of boar mince goes a long way, and that coupled with a little fresh thyme and Worcestershire sauce really does make a delicious dish.

1 Preheat the oven to 180°C/Gas 4.

2 Heat 4 tablespoons of the oil in a sauté pan, add the onions and thyme and cook for a few minutes to soften.

3 Add the mince and break up with a wooden spoon. Then cook for a few minutes, stirring well, until all the water from the onions and mince evaporates and they take on a touch of colour. Remove from the heat and leave to cool slightly.

4 Place a layer of the potato slices in the base of a baking dish, about 30cm square, so that they slightly overlap. Add a layer of onions and mince, then another layer of potato. Repeat until all the ingredients have been used up, finishing with a layer of potato.

5 Mix the Worcestershire sauce with the boiling stock or gravy, then pour in enough of it to come three-quarters of the way up the potatoes. Lightly oil the top of the potato with the remaining 2 tablespoons oil.

6 Place the dish on a baking tray and bake in the oven for 45 minutes, checking that the stock or gravy has not evaporated too much, and adding a touch more if it has.

7 At this point, lightly press the bake with a potato masher and then bake for a further 30 minutes or until nice and golden.

8 Remove from the oven and leave to cool for 20 minutes before serving. Any pickled vegetable is good here – such as red cabbage or onions – or try pickled walnuts.

Wild Boar Sausage with Wild Garlic & Watercress

MAKES 1KG
Preparation: 30 mins

800g boneless wild boar
  shoulder
1 small bunch watercress
1 small bunch wild garlic
  leaves
150g dried breadcrumbs
  (made from bread that has
  been toasted)
15g cooking salt
3g coarsely ground black pepper
50ml iced water
hog casings

This sausage is a cracker slowly cooked over charcoal on a barbecue – amazing!

1___Use a meat mincer fitted with a 8mm plate to mince the wild boar, watercress and wild garlic leaves.

2___Put the minced meat mixture into a large bowl.

3___Mix the breadcrumbs, salt and pepper together, then add to the minced meat mixture and mix together thoroughly with your hands.

4___Add the iced water and mix thoroughly again.

5___Mince the meat again, this time using a 5mm plate.

6___Stuff the mixture into hog casings and twist into 10–15cm links.

7___Refrigerate until ready to use.

Wild Boar & Honey Chipolatas

MAKES 1KG
Preparation: 30 mins

800g boneless wild boar
  shoulder
150g dried breadcrumbs
  (made from bread that has
  been toasted)
15g cooking salt
2g ground white pepper
50ml iced water
1 heaped tablespoon runny
  honey
sheep casings

The boar meat for this sausage is finely minced and stuffed into relatively thin sheep casings. The addition of honey makes the sausage ideal for breakfast and one that the kids will love too.

1___Use a meat mincer fitted with a 5mm plate to mince the wild boar.

2___Put the minced meat into a large bowl.

3___Mix the breadcrumbs, salt and pepper together, then add to the minced meat and mix together thoroughly with your hands.

4___Add the iced water and honey and mix thoroughly again.

5___Mince the meat again, this time using a 3mm plate.

6___Stuff the mixture into sheep casings and twist into 10–15cm links.

7___Refrigerate until ready to use.

Wild Boar Krakowska

MAKES 1KG
Preparation: 20–30 mins
Smoking: 1 hour 30 mins

100g boneless wild boar
  shoulder
900g wild boar haunch meat,
  completely free of fat and
  gristle, cut into 2.5cm cubes
20g curing salt
3g dextrose
2g sodium ascorbate
5g garlic powder, or you could
  use 4–5 garlic cloves, crushed
fibrous casing (man-made
  casing derived from collagen)

Traditionally, krakowska is a high-quality Polish slicing sausage that is quite heavily smoked and roasted. Making it with wild boar lifts it to another level.

1___Use a meat mincer fitted with a 5mm plate to mince the wild boar shoulder twice.
2___Put into a large bowl, add the cubed haunch meat and all the remaining ingredients, apart from the casing, and mix together thoroughly with your hands.
3___Stuff into the fibrous casing, without any air pockets, and tie off.
4___Hang in a smoker at a temperature of 55°C for about 1 hour 30 minutes.
5___Then roast in the smoker at 80°C until a core temperature of 70°C is reached.

Wild Boar Prosciutto Style

MAKES 1KG
Drying: 2–3 months

1kg wild boar haunch
1 pave for dry curing (see
  Glossary, page 218)

DRY CURE
42g curing salt (containing
  1% sodium nitrite and 0.8%
  potassium nitrate)
4g coarsely ground black
  pepper
2g garlic powder
6 dried bay leaves, finely
  chopped

Air dried hams are adored worldwide and it would be rude not to include one made from wild boar. Again, I advocate using a single muscle to cut down on curing and drying times.

1___Mix the dry cure ingredients together thoroughly and apply half to your wild boar.
2___Put into a strong plastic container and refrigerate for 10 days, turning over after 5 days.
3___Apply the second half of the cure mix to the venison, then refrigerate for a further 2 weeks, again ensuring that it is turned every 5 days.
4___Remove the wild boar from the container and wash off with lukewarm water.
5___Wrap the wild boar in the pave and tie up.
6___Hang the venison in an environment with a temperature of 12–14°C and a relative humidity of about 72–75 per cent with little airflow – a cellar or pantry would work well – until it is quite firm to the touch, when it is ready to eat. This will typically take 2–3 months.
7___Slice wafer thin to serve.

Cooked Game Salami

MAKES 1KG
Preparation: 30 mins
Smoking: 1 hour
Drying: 2 weeks

500g boneless wild boar
shoulder
500g game bird meat, for
example a mixture of
pheasant, partridge, pigeon
and duck, cut into 1cm cubes
20g curing salt
2g ground white pepper
3g dextrose
2g sodium ascorbate
fibrous casing (man-made
casing derived from
collagen), about 7.5cm in
diameter

Although this is called a salami, it doesn't exhibit that familiar fermented taste. It is a cooked product without any added water, and air-dried after cooking to intensify its flavour.

1___Use a meat mincer fitted with a 5mm plate to mince the wild boar twice.
2___Put into a large bowl, add the cubed game bird meat and all the remaining ingredients, apart from the casing, and mix together thoroughly with your hands.
3___Stuff into the fibrous casing, without any air pockets, and tie off.
4___Hang in a smoker at a temperature of 55°C for about an hour.
5___Transfer to a steam oven and steam at 80°C until a core temperature of 70°C is reached.
6___Hang the salami to air-dry in an environment with a temperature of 12–14°C and a relative humidity of about 75–80 per cent – a cellar or pantry would work well – for about 2 weeks or until it has lost 15–20 per cent in weight.

Wild Boar Lap Cheong

MAKES 1KG
Preparation: 40 mins
Smoking: 1 hour

1kg boneless wild boar
    shoulder, completely free of
    gristle and sinew
22g curing salt
20g sugar
4g garlic powder
4g Chinese five-spice powder
2g ground white pepper
1.5g ground cinnamon
2 tablespoons rice wine
100ml iced water
sheep casings

Lap cheong is a traditional smoked Chinese sausage that is usually made from fatty pork and would normally contain a lot of sugar and monosodium glutamate. My adaptation contains wild boar and no MSG while still maintaining its distinctive flavour profile.

1___Use a meat mincer fitted with a 8mm plate to mince the wild boar shoulder.
2___Put into a large bowl, add all the remaining ingredients, apart from the casings, and mix together thoroughly with your hands.
3___Stuff the mixture into sheep casings and twist into 15–20cm links.
4___Hang in a smoker at a temperature of 60°C for about an hour.
5___Then roast in the smoker at 80°C until a core temperature of 70°C is reached.
6___Hang in the fridge for about 12 hours to chill, after which the sausages should have a dark brown wrinkled appearance and be ready to eat.

Wild Boar Bacon Ayrshire Style

MAKES 1KG
Preparation: 15 mins
Curing: 4–5 days

1kg boneless wild boar middle
    (loin and belly)

BRINE
1kg chilled water
160g curing salt (containing
    0.6% sodium nitrite)
3g dextrose

Ayrshire-style bacon is typically the loin and the belly left in one piece and the belly rolled into the loin and tied. This is then cured and cut into nice big round rashers. It can be smoked if you wish, but I prefer to leave it unsmoked and serve it just slightly crispy in a fresh crusty roll.

1___Roll the belly of the wild boar into the loin and tie tightly with string.
2___Mix the cold water and salt together thoroughly in a large, deep strong plastic or stainless steel bowl or container until the salt has dissolved, then add the dextrose.
3___Put the wild boar into the brine, ensuring that it is fully immersed, and leave in the fridge for 1 week.
4___Remove the meat from the brine and dry thoroughly. I usually do this in my smoker at a temperature of 60°C for about an hour.
5___Wrap the meat in greaseproof paper and return to the fridge for a further 4–5 days to completely cure through. Then slice to your desired thickness, cook and enjoy!

3   WILDFOWL

Wildfowl

Wild duck and geese come in many shapes and forms and there are restrictions on what species you can and cannot shoot. In the UK you are allowed to shoot common pochard, gadwall, goldeneye, mallard, pintail, shoveller, teal, tufted and widgeon wild duck and Canada, greylag and pink-footed geese. You can only shoot white-fronted in England and Wales.

I have only ever cooked a few of these species of duck and only ever cooked and eaten Canada goose. But I'm told that they are pretty much the same. More important is the age of the bird; the younger the better. Older geese are mostly pretty awful, and as tough as old boots. Younger geese are nice roasted or braised slowly in a moist environment. I once had wild goose braised in red wine in Italy and it was spectacular – rich, moist and deep in flavour – but never here. This is probably due to the fact it's forbidden to sell them, so if you want to try something similar, get friendly with a wildfowler, as they'll be able to get you plenty.

Wild duck are delicious roasted, in broths and soups, braised and sometimes grilled. The fact that they are quite lean, as opposed to domestic duck, makes them attractive to professional and home cooks alike. Generally speaking, most duck will feed 2–4, apart from teal, which normally only serves 1. Geese, however, can feed up to 6 or even 8, depending on the size and age and how you cook them.

Plucking is a bit of a pain, as most wildfowl have an almost double layer of feather, an outer and finer downy under feather. And the feathers go everywhere, so you have been warned!

Roast Wild Duck with Bitter Orange Sauce

SERVES 2
Preparation: 20 mins
Cooking: 20 mins, plus resting

2 tablespoons olive oil
2 Mallard duck crowns,
   twin breasts on the bone,
   wishbones removed
salt and freshly ground black
   pepper

SAUCE
75g caster sugar
200ml freshly squeezed
   orange juice
50ml lemon juice
50ml cider vinegar
200ml duck or game stock (see
   page 214)
zest of 1 large orange, finely
   shredded into strips
15g ice-cold unsalted butter

This is a twist on duck à l'orange, a classic when I was a young boy growing up. It was one of the earliest dishes I ever cooked in my first part-time job in a pub. Even now I really like the combination – it works so well and is so simple to prepare and cook.

SAUCE

1___Put the sugar and enough water to just cover the sugar into a wide sauté pan.

2___Bring to the boil and boil rapidly until the water evaporates and the sugar starts to turn a golden brown. Now be careful here, as it will go black very quickly indeed (the darker the caramel goes, the less sweet the sauce will be).

3___When you have a nice deep brown colour, add the orange and lemon juice and the vinegar. It will splutter, so stand back.

4___Cook until the sugar and juices are amalgamated, then add the stock and reduce down over a medium heat until you have a good sauce consistency.

5___Put the orange zest into a small saucepan, cover with cold water and bring to the boil. Strain and return to the pan, then repeat twice more. This will take the bitterness out of the zest.

6___Add the zest to the sauce and mix well.

7___Finally, off the heat, swirl in the cold butter to add richness to the sauce.

DUCK

1___Preheat the oven to 220°C/Gas 7.

2___Heat the oil in an ovenproof frying pan.

3___Season the duck crowns well inside and out with salt and pepper, then place skin side down in the hot oil and cook for 1 minute.

4___Transfer straight away to the hot oven and cook for 6–8 minutes, then turn the crowns over and cook for a further 6 minutes.

5___Remove the pan from the oven (the duck will still be slightly undercooked at this stage), then turn the crowns back onto the skin, cover loosely with foil and leave to rest in a warm place for 15 minutes while you finish the sauce.

TO SERVE

1___Carve the breasts off the bone, which will be perfectly cooked, pink and delicious, and slice each side into two or three slices.

2___Place on warm plates and spoon over a little of the sauce.

Poached Salted Mallard Breast with Beetroot

SERVES 4
Preparation: 30 mins, plus marinating
Cooking: 5 mins, plus resting

2 Mallard duck crowns,
twin breasts on the bone,
wishbones removed (this
makes the breasts easier to
remove once cooked)
salt and freshly ground black
pepper

RUB

3 tablespoons sea salt
1 teaspoon freshly ground
black pepper
1 teaspoon Chinese five-spice
powder

SALAD

about 350g cooked beetroot,
cut into 5mm cubes, at room
temperature
½ small red onion, very finely
chopped
1 small celery stick, very finely
chopped
4 small gherkins, very finely
chopped
3 teaspoons yellow mustard
seeds
1 teaspoon creamed
horseradish
2 tablespoons extra virgin
olive oil

An unusual dish this, as it's not very often that you poach any red meat, and that includes game birds. But handled carefully, it can make a nice change. The secret is to get some flavour into the skin and fat, otherwise it tastes flabby and insipid. This coupled with serving the flesh pink is a surprising combination, but it really does work well. I'm a lover of beetroot in any shape or form, but it has to be at room temperature or warmer for its delicate flavour not to be lost.

1__Wash and dry the duck crowns really well.

2__Mix all the ingredients for the rub together well.

3__Rub the mixture all over the crowns on both sides, really massaging it in well. Place in a glass, ceramic or stainless steel dish, cover with clingfilm and refrigerate overnight.

4__The next day, wash the crowns well – the skin will have tightened up nicely and taken on a slightly different colour.

5__Place a saucepan of salted water on the stove and bring to the boil.

6__Once boiling, carefully slide the duck crowns in and bring back to the boil as quickly as possible. At the boiling point, turn the heat right down to a simmer and cook for 2 minutes. Remove the crowns from the pan, cover with clingfilm and leave to rest in a warm place for at least 5 minutes.

7__Mix all the ingredients for the salad together well and season with salt and pepper.

8__Remove the clingfilm from the duck crowns and place on a chopping board. Carefully slice down either side of the breastbone and carve the breast meat away from the bone. Lay the breasts on kitchen paper to drain – the meat will be beautifully pink.

9__Slice each breast piece into five or six thin slices and drain well again.

10_Serve on warm plates, piling the beetroot salad next to the sliced poached meat.

Wild Duck with Poached Sweet & Sour Quince

SERVES 4
Preparation: 30 mins, plus marinating, cooling and chilling
Cooking: about 2 hours 15 mins

2 wild ducks, dry-plucked (plucked without being plunged into water or hot wax), split in half and backbone removed

8 tablespoons sea salt

2 teaspoons freshly ground black pepper

1 whole head of garlic, chopped, including skin

2 tablespoons Madeira

3 fresh bay leaves

3 sprigs of fresh rosemary, 4cm in length

3 sprigs of fresh thyme, 4cm in length

400g duck or goose fat

700g potatoes, such as Désirée, King Edward or Maris Piper, peeled and cut into 1cm cubes

50g rocket or watercress

Sweet & Sour Quince (see recipe right), to serve

Wild duck meat is dark and packed full of flavour. It combines well with the sweetness of port and Madeira, but also the bitterness of chicory (Belgium endive) and the tartness of fruits such as Seville oranges. This idea came to me on a shoot while waiting for the ducks to fly over. I had bought a lot of quinces from the local greengrocer and had used them every which way – from pies to poaching in grapefruit tea – when I suddenly thought of making a sweet and sour version.

1__The day before, wipe the duck cavities out with kitchen paper.

2__Put the salt, pepper, garlic and Madeira into a glass bowl. Bruise the herbs with a rolling pin so that they release more flavour, add to the salt mixture and mix well.

3__Add the duck halves and coat well with the salt mixture, rubbing well into all the cavities. Cover the bowl with clingfilm and leave to marinate in a fridge for 24 hours, turning occasionally.

4__Preheat the oven to 140°C/Gas 1.

5__Wash the duck halves well under cold water and pat dry, reserving the herbs and garlic.

6__Melt the duck or goose fat in a heavy-based ovenproof sauté pan. Add the duck , along with the herbs and garlic, and heat the fat until it starts to bubble, cover with a lid and transfer to the oven. Cook the duck slowly until a knife can be inserted without any resistance. This can take up to 2 hours, but everyone's ovens are different, so start to check after about 1 hour 30 minutes. When the duck is cooked, remove from the oven and leave to cool completely, then chill.

7__Lift the duck out of the fat, rinse briefly under warm water and pat dry.

8__Heat some of the duck fat in a non-stick frying pan until very hot. Pat the potato cubes dry, then add to the hot fat, season well and cook slowly over a medium heat, stirring occasionally, for about 15–20 minutes until cooked through and they take on a nice colour.

9__Once cooked, strain in a colander and keep warm.

10_Meanwhile, heat a frying pan on the stove. Pull the legs away from the duck breast and then add all the duck pieces skin side down to the pan. Cook for about 8–10 minutes, turning once or twice, until the skin is well browned and slightly crispy and the duck is warmed through.

11_To serve, pull the duck meat off the bone and cut into even-sized pieces. Toss together with the hot seasoned potatoes.

12_Arrange a few rocket leaves or watercress sprigs on a plate, top with the hot duck and potatoes and scatter over a few cubes of the sweet and sour quince – perfect.

Sweet & Sour Quince

MAKES ONE 750ML JAR
Preparation: 10 mins, plus cooling
Cooking: 5 mins

75ml white wine vinegar
75ml perry vinegar
10 black peppercorns
75g caster sugar
1 quantity of Sweet Pickled
   Quinces (see page 218), plus
   200ml of the syrup

1___Put all the ingredients into a stainless steel saucepan and bring to the boil, then remove from the stove and leave to cool.
2___Drain the quinces well, reserving the syrup, cut into quarters and remove the core. Carefully peel off the skin, but you can leave it on if you want to.
3___Cut each quarter into uniform 2cm chunks and pack into a sterilised 750ml Kilner jar. Pour over the syrup until the quince is covered.
4___Seal and store for up to 1 month in a cool, dark place.

Roast Wild Duck with Blackberries

SERVES 2
Preparation: 5 minutes
Cooking: about 20 minutes

2 tablespoons olive oil
2 wild duck crowns, on the
   bone, skin on
salt and freshly ground black
   pepper

SAUCE
300ml red wine
600ml strong game stock (see
   page 214) or chicken stock
6 tablespoons crème de cassis
10g ice-cold unsalted butter
200g blackberries
1 tablespoon double cream
   (optional)

This is an easy duck recipe with a rich, powerful sauce. To go with it, all you'll need are a few roasted carrots and some pan-fried potatoes.

1___Preheat the oven to 220°C/Gas 7.
2___Heat the oil in an ovenproof frying pan.
3___Season the duck breasts well with salt and pepper, then place skin side down in the hot oil and brown well.
4___Transfer the pan to the oven and cook for 5–6 minutes, then turn the breasts over and cook for a further 2–3 minutes.
5___Remove the pan from the oven, then transfer the duck to a warm plate, skin side down, cover loosely with foil and leave to rest in a warm place for 10 minutes.

SAUCE
1___Meanwhile, tip away any oil from the pan, then add the red wine and boil rapidly over a high heat until almost all evaporated.
2___Add the stock and again reduce rapidly until you have a nicely thickened sauce.
3___Add the cassis and butter and whisk well, then taste and adjust the seasoning.
4___Strain the sauce through a fine sieve into a clean pan. Add the blackberries and stir well, then add the cream if using.

TO SERVE
Slice the breasts, drain on kitchen paper, place on warm plates and spoon over the sauce.

Sautéed Wild Duck Breast with Apricots, Green Peppercorns & Five Spice

SERVES 4
Preparation: 10 mins
Cooking: about 15 mins, plus resting

2–3 pinches of Chinese five-spice powder, plus extra for seasoning

4 wild duck breasts, removed from the crowns, skin side scored through the fat but not the flesh

salt and freshly ground black pepper

350g can apricots in syrup

1 tablespoon drained green peppercorns in brine, plus a few extra

1 tablespoon peppercorn brine from the jar

sugar, for seasoning

juice of 1 large lemon

2–3 tablespoons olive oil

4 pak choi, cut lengthways into quarters

2 tablespoons soy sauce

1 tablespoon mirin

Sometimes you come across a recipe that really works well with the minimum of fuss. Yes, the purists may sneer, but this recipe is so easy and when I cooked it on telly last year I had a huge response, probably one of the most popular of the year. Yes, it uses canned apricots, and yes, it uses jarred peppercorns in brine, but it works. Just because you use a can or jar doesn't mean to say that you can't get a great end result. Go on, try it!

1___Heat a dry non-stick frying pan.

2___Sprinkle the five-spice powder over the duck breasts and rub in well, then season well with salt and pepper.

3___Place skin side down in the hot pan and cook for about 6–7 minutes until the fat runs.

4___Turn over and cook for a further 2–3 minutes.

5___Remove the pan from the stove, then transfer the duck to a warm plate, cover loosely with foil and leave to rest in a warm place for 10 minutes. Do not leave for too long, otherwise it will overcook.

6___Meanwhile, put the apricots and syrup into a blender or food-processor with the peppercorns and the brine and whizz well.

7___Pour into a small bowl and season well with salt and pepper, sugar and five-spice, then add a few whole peppercorns.

8___Heat the oil in a wok or frying pan, add half the pak choi and season with a little five-spice. Sauté until slightly wilted, then add half the soy sauce and mirin and stir well.

9___Spoon into a bowl, then wipe out the pan with kitchen paper and repeat.

10_To serve, slice the duck across the grain into six or seven slices and drain well. Spoon the pak choi in the middle of a warm plate or bowl, lay the duck over and drizzle with the apricot sauce.

Sautéed Wild Duck Breasts
with Cauliflower, Banana & Ginger

SERVES 4
Preparation: 15 mins
Cooking: 15–20 mins, plus resting

salt and freshly ground black pepper

1 small cauliflower, cut into roughly 2cm florets

2 tablespoons olive oil

$\frac{1}{2}$ tablespoon chopped fresh red chilli

1 tablespoon peeled and chopped fresh ginger

2 garlic cloves, finely chopped

1 red onion, finely chopped

3 tablespoons dark soy sauce

1 large ripe banana, peeled and cut into small cubes

50g unsalted butter

breasts from 2 wild ducks, i.e. 4 individual ones, removed from the crown and neatly trimmed

This dish typifies my aspirations in developing this collection of recipes in that I really wanted to push the boundaries with game meats and see how we could move them on. Yes, I know what you're thinking, banana with game? But I really believe this works. Banana can be a difficult ingredient to match with others, especially when you're talking savoury. It needs very careful thought. Anyway, try it; I think you'll be surprised.

1___Bring a small saucepan of salted water to the boil. Plunge in the cauliflower and return to the boil for 1 minute, then drain well in a colander.

2___Heat the oil in a sauté pan, add the chilli, ginger, garlic and onion and cook for 3–4 minutes until softened.

3___Stir in the cauliflower and season well, then coat well in the chilli mixture.

4___Add the soy sauce and bring to the boil, then remove the pan from the heat. It's essential that the cauliflower does not disintegrate.

5___Off the heat, add the banana to the mixture and mix well, then keep warm.

6___Heat the butter in a non-stick frying pan until foaming and slightly brown.

7___Season the breasts well with salt and pepper, then place skin side down in the hot butter and cook for 3–4 minutes until well browned. Turn over and cook for a further 2–3 minutes. Do not overcook!

8___Remove the pan from the stove, then transfer the duck to a warm plate, cover loosely with foil and leave to rest in a warm place for a good 5 minutes.

9___To serve, spoon the cauliflower mixture into the centre of a warm deep bowl. Slice the duck breasts into 2cm cubes and scatter over the top. That's it.

Wild Duck Braised Rice
with Chilli, Cumin & Black Onion Seeds

SERVES 4
Preparation: 25 mins
Cooking: about 25 mins, plus resting

3 tablespoons any oil

2 Mallard ducks, all meat removed, including skin, and roughly chopped

8 thin bacon rashers, roughly chopped

1 medium onion, finely chopped

1 tablespoon chopped garlic

1 teaspoon chopped fresh red chilli

2 tablespoons black onion (nigella or kalonji) seeds

½ teaspoon ground cumin

8 heads of Tenderstem broccoli

freshly ground black pepper

10g good-quality chicken stock cube

150g basmati rice, washed 3 times in a sieve, then soaked in warm water for 10 minutes and drained well

about 300ml boiling water

I love all-in-one-pot dishes like this. It's so easy and you get a great result every time. But just ensure that the lid fits really well so that the rice cooks in the allocated time. Any vegetable is good here: peas, cabbage, cavalo nero or spinach.

1___Preheat the oven to 200°C/Gas 6.

2___Heat the oil in a large ovenproof sauté pan with a tight-fitting lid. Add the duck meat and bacon and sauté quickly until a nice colour has been achieved. Remove from the pan and reserve.

3___Add the onion, garlic, chilli, black onion seeds and cumin, mix well and cook for 5 minutes until the onion has softened.

4___Trim the broccoli, cutting the stalks into small pieces and leaving the heads intact.

5___Add the stalks to the onion mixture, then return the duck and bacon to the pan and really stir well.

6___Add the rice and stir to coat in the duck and onion mixture.

7___Crumble over the stock cube and stir in, then season well with pepper (no salt is needed).

8___Pour in the boiling water, stir well and bring to the boil.

9___Place the broccoli heads on top of the rice and gently push down.

10__Cover the pan with the lid, transfer to the oven and cook for 16–18 minutes, and providing the mixture is boiling, the rice will cook in this time!

11__Once cooked, remove the pan from the oven and fluff the rice up with a fork, then re-cover and leave to rest for 10 minutes.

12__Serve in warm deep bowls.

Warm Roast Duck
with Broccoli, Radishes & Anchovy

**SERVES 2 AS A MAIN;
4 AS A STARTER**
Preparation: 10 mins
**Cooking: 20 mins, plus
resting**

2 wild duck crowns, twin
   breasts on the bone,
   wishbones removed
salt and freshly ground black
   pepper
2 tablespoons olive oil
4 salted anchovy fillets, finely
   chopped or mashed to a paste
3 tablespoons roughly chopped
   fresh parsley
2 tablespoons roughly chopped
   fresh tarragon
6 tablespoons extra virgin
   olive oil
a pinch of sugar
15g rocket, finely chopped
2 tablespoons cold water
500g broccoli, trimmed,
   leaving a few leaves – split
   any thick stalks so that all are
   about the same width
150g radishes, finely sliced on
   the diagonal

I know you're thinking this sounds a bit odd, but trust me – it works. The balance here is between the saltiness of the dressing and the richness of the pink-cooked wild duck. Oddly enough, the intense fish flavour works well in this dish and has become a favourite of mine. It also goes well with roasted saddle of hare.

1___Preheat the oven to 220°C/Gas 7.

2___Heat the olive oil in an ovenproof frying pan.

3___Season the crowns inside and out with salt and pepper, then place skin side down in the hot oil and cook for 2–3 minutes until they start to colour.

4___Transfer the pan to the oven and cook for 8 minutes.

5___Meanwhile, put the anchovies, herbs, extra virgin olive oil, sugar and salt and pepper in a bowl and whisk together.

6___Turn the duck skin side up and cook for a further 4–5 minutes. Remove the pan from the oven, cover loosely with foil and leave to rest in a warm place for at least 15 minutes.

7___Add the rocket to the anchovy dressing and mix well with the water.

8___Cook the broccoli in a saucepan of salted boiling water until just tender. Drain well and keep warm.

TO SERVE

9___Arrange the warm broccoli evenly on four plates and sprinkle with the radishes.

10__Carefully slice down either side of the breastbone to remove the four breasts from the crowns and then slice each breast at an angle. Dab the cut duck meat on a piece of kitchen towel to remove any excess blood.

11__Lay the duck meat over and under the broccoli, then spoon over the dressing.

Braised Wild Goose with Herbs, Juniper & Redcurrant Jelly

SERVES 4
Preparation: 30 mins, plus cooling
Cooking: about 1 hour 25 mins

2 tablespoons any oil
4 large onions, finely chopped
4 garlic cloves, finely chopped
250g good-quality pork sausage meat
200g minced game meat – meat from the goose legs, plus any other game meat (failing that, use chicken or turkey mince)
2 tablespoons each chopped fresh rosemary, fresh tarragon and fresh thyme
salt and freshly ground black pepper
4–6 wild goose breasts, depending on size, boned, skin on
200ml red wine
500ml strong game stock (see page 214) or chicken stock
10 juniper berries, crushed
3 tablespoons redcurrant or apple jelly
2 tablespoons cornflour or arrowroot, mixed with 4 tablespoons cold water

I had wild goose braised in a deep red wine sauce in Italy some years ago. The flavour and texture were so powerful that I can still remember it now. There, it was cut into large chunks and braised long and slow for many hours. Here, I have refined it slightly, as wild geese can be slightly tougher than a domestic bird. This way of cooking ensures that the end result is delicious and full of flavour.

1___Heat the oil in a large sauté pan, add the onions and garlic and cook for 5 minutes to soften, then leave to cool.

2___Preheat the oven to 190°C/Gas 5.

3___Mix the sausage meat and game meat together well in a bowl.

4___Add the herbs and mix well, then add the cooled onions and mix well again, adding a little salt and pepper.

5___Slice each of the goose breasts into two or three long pieces on a slight angle.

6___Place each slice on a large piece of clingfilm moistened with a little water. Using a rolling pin or meat mallet, gently beat out each piece of goose breast so that it's nice and thin. Leave the fat on.

7___Repeat the process so that you have 8–12 pieces (if using four breasts).

8___Roll the sausage and game meat mixture into small cylinders, the same number as you have thin goose slices.

9___Roll these cylinders up inside the thin goose slices so that you end up with a fatter cylinder.

10__Pack the parcels tightly into a baking tray.

11__Bring the red wine and stock to the boil in a saucepan and add the juniper, salt and pepper and the redcurrant or apple jelly.

12__Pour over the parcels, then cover tightly with foil, place in the oven and cook for 1 hour 15 minutes.

13__Remove the pan from the oven and lift off the foil. Carefully tip off the gravy, using the foil to stop the parcels falling out.

14__Leave the gravy to rest for a couple of minutes, then skim off the fat and discard.

15__Add the cornflour or arrowroot mixture to the gravy and cook until slightly thickened.

16__Serve the gravy with the goose parcels, along with baby carrots and roasted parsnips.

Simply Roasted Teal

SERVES 4
Preparation: 25 mins
Cooking: about 40 mins, plus resting

2 tablespoons any oil
4 Teal ducks, dressed and wishbones removed
salt and freshly ground black pepper
2 shallots, chopped
2 garlic cloves, crushed
1 celery stick, chopped
2 star anise (optional)
2 tablespoons white wine vinegar
100ml dry white wine
300ml strong game stock (see page 214) or chicken stock
a pinch of sugar
2 teaspoons ice-cold unsalted butter

This may be a very simple recipe but it has a delicious outcome. The accompanying sauce is all the better by being made with the bones from the freshly roasted birds – really tasty.

1___Preheat the oven to 230°C/Gas 8.

2___Heat the oil in a large ovenproof frying pan.Season the birds well inside and out with salt and pepper, then place breast side down in the hot oil and cook for 2–3 minutes until well sealed, ensuring that both breasts are nicely coloured.

3___Turn the birds over so that they are sitting on their backs and transfer the pan to the oven to roast hard for 10 minutes. At the 10-minute point, check to see if the birds are well coloured but not overcooked – the breast meat should still be slightly soft when lightly pressed.

4___Remove the pan from the oven and transfer the birds to a warm tray, turning them back onto their breasts. Loosely cover with foil and leave to rest in a warm place for at least 10 minutes.

5___When the birds have rested, transfer to a chopping board. First, remove the legs of one bird. Using a sharp knife, slice through the skin where the leg is attached to the breast, then pull the leg back on itself so that the ball and socket joint pops open and carefully pull the leg away.

6___Carefully slice down one side of the breastbone, continuing to cut right along to the wing, then cut through the wing joint. Tease the flesh away from the crown and gently pull the breast meat away. Repeat on the other side.Cover the legs and breast meat with foil and keep warm while you repeat with the other three birds.

7___Place the frying pan back on the stove and add the shallots, garlic, celery and star anise, if using.

8___Chop up the carcasses into small pieces, add to the frying pan and cook over a fairly high heat for about 10 minutes until the bones and veg have taken on some colour.

9___Add the vinegar and boil rapidly over a high heat until almost all evaporated.

10__Add the wine and boil, scraping off all the lovely caught bits from the pan.

11__Pour the contents of the frying pan into a small saucepan, add the stock and bring to the boil, then reduce the heat, skim and simmer for 10 minutes.

12__When ready to serve, strain the stock, season well with salt and pepper and add the sugar. It should be well reduced by now. Add the butter and swirl in to give the sauce a nice shine.

13__Place the roasted teal (you may have to flash it through the hot oven) in a hot serving bowl and pour over the well-reduced sauce.

Teal Broth with Mushrooms, Sherry & Spinach

SERVES 2
Preparation: 30 mins
Cooking: 20 mins

2 Teal ducks, dressed

750ml game stock (see page 214)

4 small shallots, very finely sliced

200ml dry sherry

3 tablespoons dark soy sauce

150g chestnut or open cap mushrooms, finely sliced

salt and freshly ground black pepper

50g baby spinach leaves

2 tablespoons full-flavoured extra virgin olive oil

Teal need very little cooking and the secret here is to poach the breast only, to avoid overcooking it. The thighs need a little longer and the drumsticks are really just used for flavour. Like any good soup, it's only as good as the base stock, so if yours is a little weak, gently reduce slightly by simmering to increase the flavour and colour. Sherry was always served in and/or with consommé when I was a young chef but seems to have gone out of fashion. The addition of some really punchy, peppery, herby olive oil is delicious – the aroma when warmed is fabulous.

1___Place one duck on a chopping board. Slice down the breastbone, and carefully cut one breast away from the bone. Remove the fat. Repeat with the other side. Cut each breast into six or eight pieces. Repeat with the other duck.

2___Slice off the legs, then remove the skin. Chop the thigh meat only, leaving the drumsticks whole.

3___Place the stock in a saucepan and add the chopped thigh meat and drumsticks with the shallots, sherry and soy sauce, then bring to the boil. Turn the heat down and simmer for 15 minutes.

4___Skim off any fat that has risen to the surface and then remove the drumsticks and discard. Add the teal breast and mushrooms, then simmer for 4 minutes.

5___Quickly remove from the heat and season well with salt and pepper.

6___To serve, place the spinach leaves in warm deep bowls and spoon in the teal broth, then spoon ½ tablespoon olive oil onto each serving of broth. It's as simple as that.

Roasted Teal Stuffed with Ceps & Garlic

SERVES 4
Preparation: 30 mins, plus cooling
Cooking: about 25 mins, plus resting

4 Teal ducks, dressed and
 wishbones removed
2 tablespoons any oil

STUFFING
75g unsalted butter
4 large garlic cloves, finely
 chopped
3 large ceps, cleaned
4 tablespoons chopped fresh
 parsley
salt and freshly ground black
 pepper

Teal paired with beautiful ceps fried in a little butter with garlic and parsley: a great recipe that pretty much sums up the highlights of autumn. I sometimes serve a little mashed potato on the side, which is all you really need.

STUFFING

1___Heat the butter in a saucepan until just foaming and turning a light brown colour. Add the garlic and cook for 2–3 minutes until lightly coloured.

1___Add the ceps and gently fry so that they also take on a little colour, but only partly cook. Spoon the contents of the pan into a bowl.

1___Add the parsley and salt and pepper and mix well.

TEAL

1___Preheat the oven to 230°C/Gas 8.

2___Stuff the birds equally with the cep and garlic mixture.

3___Secure the stuffing in place with a cocktail stick or use string to tie the legs together.

4___Heat the oil in a large ovenproof frying pan, then place the birds breast side down in the hot oil and cook for 2–3 minutes until well sealed, ensuring that both breasts are nicely coloured.

5___Turn the birds over so that they are sitting on their backs and transfer the pan to the oven to roast hard for 10 minutes.

6___At the 10-minute point, check to see if the birds are well coloured but not overcooked – the breast meat should still be slightly soft when lightly pressed.

7___Remove the pan from the oven and transfer the birds to a warm tray, turning them back onto their breasts. Loosely cover with foil and leave to rest in a warm place for at least 10 minutes.

8___When the birds have rested, transfer to a chopping board. First, remove the legs of one bird. Using a sharp knife, slice through the skin where the leg is attached to the breast, then pull the leg back on itself so that the ball and socket joint pops open and carefully pull the leg away.

9___Carefully slice down one side of the breastbone, continuing to cut right along to the wing, then cut through the wing joint. Tease the flesh away from the crown and gently pull the breast meat away. Repeat on the other side.

10___Cover the legs and breast meat with foil and keep warm while you repeat with the other three birds.

11___Serve the legs and breast meat in warm deep bowls with the buttery stuffing to one side.

Roasted Teal with Pickled Autumn Raspberries

SERVES 4
Preparation: 35 mins, plus cooling
Cooking: about 45 mins, plus resting

2 tablespoons any oil
4 Teal ducks, dressed and
   wishbones removed
salt and freshly ground black
   pepper
2 shallots, chopped
2 garlic cloves, crushed
1 celery stick, chopped
2 star anise (optional)
2 tablespoons white wine
   vinegar
50ml dry white wine
300ml strong game stock (see
   page 214) or chicken stock
a pinch of sugar
2 teaspoons ice-cold unsalted
   butter
50ml framboise liqueur

PICKLED RASPBERRIES
200g fresh autumn raspberries
100ml fresh apple juice
3 tablespoons runny honey
2 tablespoons balsamic or
   sherry vinegar
2 pinches of salt
a pinch of freshly grated
   nutmeg

The raspberries must be very ripe and full of flavour for this dish to work successfully. The pickle is a very light one, and the berries are perfect to eat after just a few hours. Adding a touch of raspberry liqueur to the finished sauce gives it a sweet, fruity edge that goes perfectly with the teal.

PICKLED RASPBERRIES

1___Put the raspberries into a small ceramic bowl or glass preserving jar.

2___Put all the other ingredients into a stainless steel saucepan and bring to the boil, then reduce the heat and simmer for 2 minutes.

3___Remove from the heat and leave to cool for 10 minutes, then pour over the raspberries and leave to cool to room temperature. Serve after an hour or two or pop in the fridge where they will keep for a week or so but will lose a little colour.

TEAL

1___When ready to cook, preheat the oven to 230°C/Gas 8.

2___Heat the oil in a large ovenproof frying pan. Season the teal well inside and out, then place breast side down in the hot oil and cook for 2–3 minutes until well sealed, ensuring that both breasts are nicely coloured. Turn the birds over so that they are sitting on their backs and transfer the pan to the oven for 10 minutes.

3___At the 10-minute point, check to see if the birds are well coloured but not overcooked – the breast meat should still be slightly soft when lightly pressed.

4___Remove the pan from the oven and transfer the birds to a warm tray, turning them back onto their breasts. Loosely cover with foil and leave to rest in a warm place for at least 10 minutes.

5___Transfer the birds to a chopping board. Using a sharp knife, slice through the skin where the leg is attached to the breast, then pull the leg back on itself so that the ball and socket joint pops open and carefully pull the leg away. Carefully slice down one side of the breastbone, continuing to cut right along to the wing, then cut through the wing joint. Tease the flesh away from the crown and gently pull the breast meat away. Repeat on the other side.Cover the legs and breast meat with foil and keep warm while you repeat with the other three birds.

6___Place the frying pan back on the stove and add the shallots, garlic, celery and star anise, if using.

7___Chop up the carcasses into small pieces, add to the frying pan and cook over a fairly high heat for about 10 minutes until the bones and veg have taken on some colour.

8___Add the vinegar and boil rapidly over a high heat until almost all evaporated.

9___Add the wine and boil, scraping off all the lovely caught bits from the pan.

10_Pour the contents of the frying pan into a small saucepan, add the stock and bring to the boil, then reduce the heat, skim and simmer for 10 minutes.

11_When ready to serve, strain the stock, season well with salt and pepper and add the sugar. It should be well reduced by now. Add the butter with the framboise and swirl in to give the sauce a nice shine.

12_Place the roasted teal (you may have to flash it through the hot oven) in a hot serving bowl and pour over the well-reduced sauce. Serve with the pickled raspberries.

4   FISH

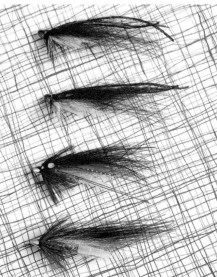
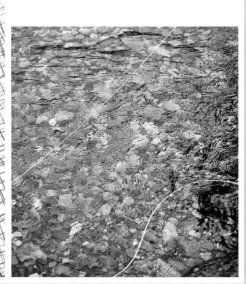

Fish

Fishing is one of the few activities to bring out the hunter-gatherer instinct. As a boy, I vividly recall sitting by canals and rivers transfixed by my fishing float, just waiting for the moment it disappeared from sight, signalling that I had a bite. Those first few seconds of not knowing quite what it is you have hooked are, until you've experienced them yourself, indescribable. For me, landing the fish was almost incidental, as I knew I would be putting it back.

In my mid twenties a friend introduced me to the noble art of fly fishing. It took me a good while to master the casting technique, but my perseverance paid off and it wasn't long before I was enjoying the magical feeling of a fish taking my fly. As I got older, my attention turned from stillwater fly fishing to fishing on a river for wild trout and salmon. I have since spent a good amount of time fishing in Scottish rivers for the king of fish, the Atlantic salmon. I have also been on a fishing trip to the west coast of Canada in search of the mighty Pacific salmon. Wherever you fish, the experience of a wild fish, one that has perhaps travelled a thousand miles to breed in the river where it was born, taking an artificial fly you had chucked in front of it takes some beating.

Tight lines. *Simon*

SALMON

In years gone by, our rivers teemed with Atlantic salmon returning to breed in the same exact place they were born, but with netting at river mouths and fisherman killing everything they caught, the population declined to frighteningly low levels. Now, however, through the help of organisations such as the Atlantic Salmon Trust, the cessation of netting and fish farming supplying much of the salmon that appears on our tables, our wild stocks are beginning to show signs of recovery. In my view, though, wild Pacific salmon, which return to their native rivers in much greater numbers, still provide a far more sustainable option than their Atlantic cousins. *Simon*

Japanese-style Grilled Marinated Alaska Sockeye Salmon with Fresh Mint & Tomato Chutney

SERVES 4
Preparation: 30 mins, plus cooling and marinating
Cooking: 15 mins

4 x 175g Alaskan sockeye
   salmon fillets

CHUTNEY
60g fresh mint leaves, washed
   well and finely chopped
2 large ripe tomatoes, chopped
2 heaped teaspoons chopped
   fresh green chilli
2 garlic cloves, finely chopped
2 tablespoons olive oil
finely grated zest and juice
   from 1 large unwaxed lime
salt and freshly ground black
   pepper

SAUCE
200ml mirin
150ml soy sauce
1 tablespoon brown miso paste
1 tablespoon toasted sesame oil
2 tablespoons caster sugar
2 tablespoons sherry vinegar

The flavours here are really powerful. The salmon is sweet and succulent, while the chutney is minty and powerful, but together they are very well matched. If you can leave the salmon to marinate overnight, all the better. I cook the salmon in the marinade and then cook down the rest of the marinade that is left over to use as a dipping sauce.

1___Put all the ingredients for the chutney into a glass or ceramic bowl, season with salt and pepper and mix well. Cover the bowl with clingfilm and chill until ready to serve.

2___Add all the ingredients for the sauce to a saucepan, mix together well and then bring to the boil.

3___Reduce the heat and simmer until you have roughly 150ml left.

4___Remove from the heat and leave to cool.

5___Pour half the cooled sauce over the salmon in a shallow glass, ceramic or stainless steel dish, cover the dish with clingfilm and leave to marinate in the fridge overnight, or a minimum of 1 hour at a pinch.

6___When ready to cook the salmon, preheat the grill to its hottest setting.

7___Lift the salmon out of the dish, leaving a little sauce on the fish, then place on a baking tray or in an ovenproof dish.

8___Cook for 6–8 minutes, depending on the temperature of the grill or until the salmon is just cooked – it's best left slightly undercooked.

9___Meanwhile, boil the remaining sauce in a saucepan.

10__Serve the salmon hot with the sauce for dipping, along with the chutney.

Grilled Wild Salmon with Figs & Red Wine

SERVES 4
Preparation: 10 mins
Cooking: about 20 mins,
plus resting

8 ripe figs

600g salmon fillet, skin on and
  scaled, cut into 4cm cubes

2–3 tablespoons olive oil

salt and freshly ground black
  pepper

GLAZE

150ml red wine

10g good-quality fish stock
  cube, crumbled

4 tablespoons balsamic
  vinegar

4 tablespoons olive oil

3 teaspoons caster sugar

1 tablespoon chopped fresh dill

Cooking wild salmon can be quite difficult, due to the fact that it is very lean and will dry out if overcooked. So always undercook and leave to rest for the best results. This recipe is quite unusual but works well. The red wine glaze is used almost as a seasoning, so a little will go a long way – probably just a teaspoon would suffice over each grilled fig and piece of salmon.

1___Cut slits in the tops of the figs, cutting roughly one-third of the way down.

2___Put all the ingredients for the glaze, apart from the dill, into a saucepan, season with salt and pepper and simmer until reduced to about one-third of its original volume. Keep warm.

3___Preheat the grill to its hottest setting.

4___Arrange the figs on the oiled tray and grill for about a minute or two only, just until soft, then remove from the heat and keep at room temperature.

6___Heat the oil in a large ovenproof frying pan.

7___Season the salmon well with salt and pepper, then place skin side down into the hot pan and cook for 2–3 minutes.

8___Place the pan under the grill (or alternatively into an oven preheated to 200°C/Gas 6) and cook for 3–4 minutes. It's essential that you do not overcook the fish, so half-cook and then remove the pan from the heat, cover loosely with foil and leave to rest in a warm place for at least 5 minutes to finish cooking.

9___When ready to serve, arrange the figs in a warm deep bowl or on a warm plate and place the salmon in between the figs.

10__Stir the chopped dill into the glaze and spoon over the salmon and figs.

OYSTER

I first tried oysters with my dad, who loves them, near Blackpool in the late 1960s and have eaten them ever since in pretty much all the countries I have visited or filmed in over the years. Britain is well known for its native oysters and from Whitstable to Colchester, Mersea to Fowey, Lindisfarne to Stranraer, all produce a fabulous oyster. The Romans liked them so much they transported them from the UK to Rome (though I'm not sure I would've eaten an oyster transported that far in those days). There was a time when they were so highly prized, they were used as a currency I'm not a fan of cooking them, if I'm honest. The iodine packed freshwater kick seems to get lost when heat is applied. I tend to eat mine fresh, straight from the shell, with a little shallot vinegar and a dash of pepper. Every oyster tastes different, some are sweeter, some are fuller, some are creamier, and some saltier than others. Just remember that oysters should be eaten impeccably fresh. Also stored deep shell down in wet seaweed or newspaper to keep the juices in.

Simple Oyster Soup

SERVES 4
Preparation: 20 mins
Cooking: 10 mins

12 fresh oysters, native or pacific, shucked and juice reserved
200ml strong fish stock
freshly ground black pepper
600ml whipping cream
8 tablespoons finely chopped fresh chives

I have never been a fan of cooking oysters, purely because I think they are so delicious on their own. I also think you lose that lovely fresh iodine flavour. Having said that, I did enjoy a Cajun *po boy* sandwich in the US last year. Here, I just boil the cream and stock, then pour it over raw oysters. It's fresh and packed full of flavour.

1___Strain the oyster juice through a very fine sieve

2___Heat the fish stock in a saucepan until it is boiling, then reduce the heat and simmer for 1 minute. Remove the pan from the stove.

3___Meanwhile, place all the oysters and juice into a blender or food-processor with a touch of pepper.

4___Now re-boil the fish stock, then add cream and bring back to the boil.

5___Start the blender or food-processor and turn to high speed. Whizz the oysters for 15–20 seconds.

6___While still blending, carefully pour in the boiling cream and fish stock mixture through the feed tube.

7___Once all the liquid has been added, leave to stand for 1 minute.

8___Straight away, pour into the four warm bowls, top with the chives and serve. That's it, no salt, just as it is.

Lightly Jellied Oysters
with Tomato, Tarragon & Gin

SERVES 4
Preparation: 30 mins, plus chilling
Cooking: 5 mins

12 large fresh oysters, native
   or pacific
2 small sheets of leaf gelatine
   (4g), soaked in cold water for
   5 minutes until very soft
4 large ripe tomatoes
2 tablespoons fresh tarragon
   leaves
50g keta (salmon) caviar
   (optional)
50ml gin
juice of 1 large lemon

TO SERVE
4 lemon wedges
cayenne pepper

Quite an odd taste combination here, but it really does work well. The jelly needs to be served ice cold straight from the fridge. All you need is a good squeeze of lemon and a dash of cayenne pepper on top just before you serve.

1   Shuck the oysters, or get a friendly fishmonger to do it for you, but keep all the juice.

2   Strain the oyster juice through a very fine sieve and measure. You will need 150ml of juice. If you fall short, add water to make up to 150ml.

3   Drain and squeeze out the excess water from the softened gelatine, then put into a small saucepan and add a couple of tablespoons of the oyster juice. Warm until the gelatine melts completely.

4   Next, bring a small saucepan of water to the boil. Remove the green stem and core from each tomato and make a small cross in the top. Plunge each of the tomatoes into the boiling water for a few seconds until the skin comes away, then plunge into cold water.

5   Carefully peel away the skins of the tomatoes. Cut each tomato into quarters and remove and discard the seeds, core and watery flesh. Cut the firm flesh that's left into small cubes and reserve.

6   Place each oyster in a shot glass or sherry schooner.

7   Distribute the tomato pieces evenly on top of the oysters.

8   Place a couple of fresh tarragon leaves and the keta caviar, if using, on top of the tomatoes.

9   Quickly stir the melted gelatine into the remaining oyster juice, then add the gin and lemon juice and mix well.

10 Pour evenly into the 12 glasses, cover the glasses with clingfilm and chill well for a minimum of 2 hours or until lightly jellied.

11 Serve with lemon wedges and a sprinkle of cayenne pepper.

SEA TROUT

Sea trout are basically brown trout that have adopted an anadromous lifestyle, whereby they go to sea to feed and return to the river to spawn, just like salmon. They are revered by fly anglers and chefs alike for their beautiful appearance and extremely delicate flavour.

However, the same issues that surround salmon also apply to sea trout, but with aquaculture also providing sea trout for the table wild stocks stand a chance of flourishing once again. *Simon*

Sea Trout with Ginger, Lime & Walnut Oil

SERVES 4
Preparation: 30 mins, plus standing and marinating

600g skinned and pin-boned
  sea trout fillet

MARINADE
2 tablespoons peeled and very
  finely grated fresh ginger
finely grated zest and juice of 4
  large unwaxed limes
2 tablespoons cider vinegar
1 tablespoon Dijon mustard
2 large garlic cloves, crushed
about 100ml extra virgin olive
  oil
1 tablespoon walnut oil
2 teaspoons caster sugar
salt and ground white pepper

TO SERVE
cracked black pepper
100g lamb's lettuce
slices of buttered brown bread

A cracking cold raw dish to serve as a starter or even a light summer main course, this is very simple to prepare and serve, and preserves the wonderful fresh taste of the sea trout. The fish, though, needs to be impeccably fresh. If you cannot get hold of walnut oil, then extra virgin olive oil will be fine on its own. The ginger must be very finely grated so that you get a mush, not small pieces of ginger. I use a Microplane for this, which is perfect for the job.

1___Put the ginger, lime zest and juice, vinegar, mustard and garlic into a large glass or ceramic bowl and whisk really well.

2___Add the oils, sugar and salt and white pepper, and really mix well again.

3___Leave the marinade to stand for 20 minutes at room temperature. It's now ready for the trout.

4___Slice the sea trout on a slight angle 5mm thick.

5___Put the trout into a glass, ceramic or stainless steel dish. Spoon over the marinade, ensuring that it coats all the fish, including the underside. Cover the dish with clingfilm and leave to marinate in the fridge for 1 hour.

6___Re-coat the fish with the marinade – the flesh will have turned slightly opaque.

7___Remove the dish from the fridge and bring to room temperature.

8___Serve the sea trout sprinkled with cracked black pepper, along with the lamb's lettuce and buttered brown bread.

Pan-fried Sea Trout
with Fresh Basil & Tomato Fondue Sauce

SERVES 4
Preparation: 40 mins
Cooking: 10–15 mins

75g unsalted butter

4 x 250g pieces of sea trout, or small fillets, skin on, scaled and pin-boned

salt and freshly ground black pepper

SAUCE

6 large ripe well-perfumed tomatoes, cut in half, plus 1 medium tomato

1 teaspoon tomato purée

1 tablespoon sherry vinegar

2–3 tablespoons cold water

50g ice-cold butter, diced

6 tablespoons extra virgin olive oil

sugar, for seasoning

4 tablespoons roughly chopped fresh basil

I'm not sure why this sauce is called tomato fondue – it's just what I was told years ago. In any case, it's simple but with a powerful, fresh flavour. The secret is not to warm the base too much, so that you keep that lovely freshness. The delicate sea trout flesh needs very careful cooking, so undercook it and then leave it to rest.

SAUCE BASE

1___Put the tomatoes into a blender with the tomato purée, vinegar and water and whizz to a fine purée, then push through a really fine sieve into a saucepan. Season lightly and mix well. Set aside.

2___Put the kettle on to boil and, meanwhile, remove the green stem from the medium tomato, make a small cross in the top and then put it into a large mug. Pour over the boiling water and leave for 20 seconds until the skin starts to peel away.

3___Tip out the boiling water and refill with cold. After 20 seconds, lift out the tomato and carefully peel away the skin. Cut into quarters and remove and discard the seeds, core and watery flesh. Cut the flesh that's left into small cubes and reserve.

SEA TROUT

1___Heat the unsalted butter in a large frying pan until foaming.

2___Make four or five long incisions just through the skin of the sea trout – don't cut too deeply. Season on both sides, place in the foaming butter, skin side down, and cook for 2–3 minutes. Turn over – the skin should be a really nice colour – and cook for a further minute or two, no longer. The centre of the fish should still be raw.

3___Lift out of the pan onto a warm plate, cover loosely with foil and leave to rest in a warm place for at least 5 minutes for the residual heat to just permeate through but not fully cook the fish.

SAUCE

1___Gently heat the sauce base over a very low heat. This is very important; if you overheat it, you will lose the unique freshness of the tomatoes. When just warm, remove the pan from the heat and gradually add the cold butter, whisking all the time so that it melts and thickens the sauce. Add the oil and continue whisking – you may need to just place over the heat again, but take care.

2___Taste, season well, and a little sugar to balance the acidity. When you are happy with the result, add the basil and small cubes of tomato.

TO SERVE

Serve the fish in warm deep bowls with the warm sauce spooned over. A small green salad and a few simply boiled baby new potatoes are all you need to accompany the dish.

BROWN TROUT

Wild brown trout are a wily fish and can be very difficult to catch. I have only ever caught two in my life, but remember them really well. There is something quite magnificent, even exciting, about seeing brown trout in a stream or river. Move too quickly and they are gone! Generally speaking, most river brown trout weigh up to 450g or slightly over that.

Having said that, the British rod caught record is about 14kg. They fight like mad, so much so you think you have a monster on the line, until you land it and discover it's nothing out of the ordinary. The flesh is superb, and I generally like to cook them whole as filleting really is a waste of time.

Grilled Brown Trout with Sorrel Cream

SERVES 4
Preparation: 15 mins
Cooking: about 20 mins

butter, for greasing
4 brown trout, gutted, scaled and fins removed with a sharp pair of scissors
salt and freshly ground black pepper

SAUCE

1 small bunch fresh sorrel, about 100g
2 small shallots, finely chopped
2 teaspoons Dijon mustard
100ml dry white wine
50ml white wine vinegar
150g ice-cold unsalted butter, diced

Brown trout vary in size quite considerably depending on where they come from. True wild brown trout can grow into substantial specimens, but the ones I have cooked have always been more like brook trout, with a maximum weight of slightly over 500g. This makes a perfect meal for one person and the sweet, firm flesh is a real joy. Their small size means that filleting the fish is bit of a waste of time. Just barbecue, grill, bake or fry whole and tuck in.

1___Preheat the grill to its hottest setting.

2___Lightly butter a baking tray. Season the fish inside, place on the tray and butter the outside of the fish, then season well.

3___Rip the sorrel leaves from the stalks and roughly chop. Finely chop the stalks and put into a saucepan. Add the shallots, mustard, wine, vinegar and salt and pepper and bring to the boil. Cook until reduced by three-quarters.

4___Meanwhile, place the fish under the hot grill and cook for 6–8 minutes. Carefully turn the fish over and cook for a further 3–4 minutes until slightly undercooked.

___Remove from the grill, cover loosely with foil and leave to rest in a warm place while you finish the sauce.

5___Strain out the stalks and shallots, place the liquor in a small saucepan and bring to the boil. Add the sorrel leaves and 50g of the butter and whisk well. The sorrel will change colour and the butter will homogenise nicely with the reduction.

6___Remove from the heat and whisk in the remaining 100g butter, a little at a time, until you have a delicious glossy sauce.

7___Serve the fish on a warm plate with the sorrel butter sauce poured over.

Whole Poached Brown Trout
with Shaved Fennel & Lemon Capers

SERVES 4
Preparation: 35 mins, plus standing
Cooking: about 20 mins, plus cooling and optional chilling

4 small whole brown trout, gutted, scaled and fins removed with a sharp pair of scissors
extra virgin olive oil, for brushing
sea salt and cracked back pepper

BOUILLON
white wine vinegar
white wine
a few bay leaves
1 small bunch fresh parsley
1 small onion, finely chopped
2 celery sticks, finely chopped
1 small leek, split, washed well and finely chopped

SALAD
2 small fennel bulbs
juice of 1 large lemon
4 tablespoons extra virgin olive oil
4 tablespoons chopped fresh chives, about 2cm in length
4 tablespoons salted capers, rinsed well, drained and roughly chopped
sea salt and cracked black pepper

Another simple but really nice way to cook brown trout, this dish can be eaten hot, warm or cold. The salad benefits from being made and left for around 20 minutes to soften nicely. It's quite hard to give exact quantities for the cooking bouillon, as it depends on the size of the fish and that of your cooking vessel. But if you work on the proportions of 10 per cent vinegar, 10 per cent wine and 80 per cent water, plus the aromatics and salt and pepper, you won't go far wrong.

BOUILLON AND TROUT
1___Put all the ingredients for the bouillon into a large saucepan or deep baking tray with the appropriate proportion of water and bring to the boil, then reduce the heat and simmer for 10 minutes.
2___At the 10-minute point, drop in the fish and bring back to the boil.
3___Remove the pan from the stove carefully and leave to cool for at least 20 minutes if you want to eat the dish hot. If not, cover and cool completely, then chill in the stock, preferably overnight.
4___When ready to eat, remove the fish from the liquor and place on a plate. Using a sharp knife, peel away the skin and head.
5___Arrange the fish on a serving plate, brush with extra virgin olive oil and add a dusting of sea salt and cracked black pepper.

SALAD
1___Use a Japanese mandolin, if you have one, to shave the fennel bulbs as finely as possible.
2___Put the shaved fennel into a bowl, add all the remaining ingredients and really mix well.
3___Cover the bowl with clingfilm and leave to stand for at least 20 minutes to soften the raw fennel.

TO SERVE
Serve the fish with the fennel salad.

EEL

All eels, the theory goes, are born in the Sargasso Sea. They then spend three years returning to the rivers their parents inhabited, maturing then swimming back again! Now that's some life. There are those that say this hasn't been proven, but I quite like the story. Eel meat is highly prized around the world, though many eels that are eaten today have been farmed in Holland and then 'finished' in various countries. The UK, along with Japan, Sweden, Poland, Denmark and China eat huge amounts, so we need to be careful, as eel stocks are believed to be in decline. Smoked eel is a great delicacy and I personally love it. Its smoky, creamy flavour is a joy and when just warmed tastes even better. Good old jellied eels I also like very much. Again, it's the creaminess of the flesh that I find so tasty.

Warmed Smoked Eel
with Asparagus & Horseradish Dressing

SERVES 4
Preparation: 15 mins
Cooking: 5–6 mins

20 young asparagus spears, trimmed
olive oil, for oiling and brushing
salt and freshly ground black pepper
4 x 85g oak-smoked eel fillets

SAUCE
6 tablespoons crème fraîche
4 tablespoons chopped fresh chives
3 tablespoons mayonnaise
2 tablespoons hot horseradish sauce
dash of white wine vinegar or water, if needed

TO SERVE
20g watercress
sea salt and cracked black pepper

Another example of a few quality ingredients put together carefully and thoughtfully, resulting in a great starter or main course. Do not overcook the asparagus, and just warm the eel so that its natural oils are released.

1___Preheat the grill to its hottest setting.
3___Place the asparagus spears on an oiled baking tray, then season well with salt and pepper and brush well with olive oil.
4___Place under the hot grill and cook for about 3–4 minutes until well coloured but not overcooked.
5___Remove the asparagus from the tray and keep warm.
6___Mix all the ingredients for the sauce together in a bowl until smooth and creamy – you may need to add a dash of vinegar or water to let it down slightly.
7___Lay the eel fillets on the baking tray and cook rapidly under the hot grill until warmed through – do not overcook!

TO SERVE
1___Lay a few sprigs of watercress on the centre of each plate, top with the warm asparagus and finally top with the warm eel.
2___Spoon over a little of the horseradish sauce and add a sprinkling of cracked black pepper and sea salt. Serve straight away.

CHAR

My first encounter with this lovely fish was in the early 1980s when I worked in the English Lakes (Lake District) in Cumbria, North West England. I had never heard of it before, let alone cooked with it, although the English have in fact been cooking it for hundreds of years and even Mrs Beeton used it. But after contacting the Windermere, Ambleside & District Angling Association, I was saddened to hear that, yes, a few local guys fish for them, but it's fast becoming a conservation fish. Nets are banned and

have been for some time, and line fishing only is allowed.

However, Arctic char, which is pretty good, can be sourced from outside the UK – it's now farmed in quite a few countries, notably Iceland and Canada, and be bought frozen all year round. This farmed variety is slightly different from our native char, being larger and with a redder skin, but it still cooks and pots beautifully. Trout can be used as a substitute, as can the zander, also known as pike-perch (see page 203), or even standard perch.

Pan-fried Char with Salsify & Basil

SERVES 2
Preparation: 30 mins
Cooking: about 1 hour

400g whole salsify, washed, peeled and cut into 4cm pieces
olive oil, to cover
salt and freshly ground black pepper
2 sprigs of fresh thyme
4 garlic cloves, crushed, plus another clove, very finely chopped
1 large bunch fresh basil
2 x 200g fillets or pieces of char, depending on their size

1___The salsify can be prepared the day before and reheated, cutting down the cooking time on the day to about 15 minutes. Preheat the oven to 180°C/Gas 4.

2___Put the salsify into a small deep ovenproof dish or baking tin.

3___Heat enough olive oil to cover the salsify in a saucepan on the stove, adding salt and pepper, the thyme, crushed garlic and the stalks from the bunch of basil.

4___Carefully pour over the salsify, cover the dish or tin with foil and cook in the oven for 35–40 minutes until a knife can be inserted with no resistance.

5___Chop the basil leaves.

6___Strain the salsify well and lift out the basil stalks.

7___Heat 3–4 tablespoons of the salsify oil in a small frying pan, add the salsify and gently brown in the hot oil. This will take only 4–5 minutes, so be careful.

8___Meanwhile, heat another couple of tablespoons of the salsify in a separate frying pan.

9___Season the char fillets well with salt and pepper, add to the hot oil and sauté for 2–3 minutes on each side. Do not overcook.

10__While the char is cooking, add the chopped basil and very finely chopped garlic to the salsify, along with plenty of pepper and a little salt. Sauté briefly.

11__Serve the char with a nice pile of the salsify alongside.

Braised Char with Tomatoes & Saffron Potatoes

SERVES 2
Preparation: 20 mins
Cooking: about 20 mins

85g unsalted butter

2 small whole char, about 450g
  each, gutted and scaled but
  head on

salt and freshly ground black
  pepper

juice of 1 large lemon

20 baby Charlotte potatoes,
  peeled and halved

about 300ml good-flavoured
  fish stock

a small pinch of saffron
  threads

2 large shallots, finely chopped

TOMATOES

2 teaspoons balsamic vinegar

2 tablespoons olive oil

1 teaspoon caster sugar

8 plum tomatoes

I once had a dish like this in Norway, although they used small cod instead, and it tasted so good. I remember thinking how good a few ingredients could taste and then of course realised that the freshness of the fish made all the difference. I'm not a huge lover of saffron, as I think it can overpower a dish so easily. But it's fine if used with a little care and can contribute a particular flavour and colour that no other ingredient can match.

1___Preheat the oven to 220°C/Gas 7.

2___Heat 55g of the butter in an ovenproof frying pan until foaming.

3___Check over the char for any remaining scales, then season the fish well with salt and pepper, add to the pan skin side down and cook carefully for about 2–3 minutes until the skin has browned lightly.

4___Turn the fish over, spoon over the butter and juices and squeeze over the lemon juice.

5___Transfer the pan to the oven and cook for about 8–10 minutes, basting regularly with the juices – do not allow to overcook.

6___Meanwhile, cook the potatoes in a saucepan of boiling salted water for about 4 minutes.

7___Drain and return to the pan, pour over the fish stock and add the saffron, shallots and the remaining 30g butter.

8___Season with salt and pepper, then bring to a simmer and cook for about 10–12 minutes until the potatoes are tender and have absorbed the stock, leaving you with a thick saffron glaze.

TOMATOES

1___While the potatoes are simmering, mix the vinegar, oil and sugar together, and season with salt and pepper.

2___Cut the tomatoes in half lengthways, arrange cut side up on a baking tray and spoon over the dressing.

3___Pop into the hot oven and cook for 6–8 minutes until tomatoes are soft and tender – do not overcook. Keep warm until ready to serve.

TO SERVE

When the fish are cooked, serve whole with the saffron potatoes on the side, along with the tomato salad.

CARP

In the UK, carp has suffered from a reputation for tasting 'muddy'. Things have since changed and it's generally now farmed in clean water so is consequently of pretty good quality. The Chinese have always eaten carp and regard it as highly nutritious and beneficial. My good friend Ken Hom, the master of Chinese cooking, adores carp and loves to cook with it. It's also eaten and revered in many Eastern European countries, where it's a speciality served on Christmas Eve. So with all this in mind, I thought I would include a couple of dishes to whet your appetite and encourage you to try it.

Whole Baked Carp & Warm Aubergine & Potato Salad with Almond Pesto

SERVES 4
Preparation: 30 mins
Cooking: about 35 mins

6 tablespoons olive oil
1 medium whole carp, about
  1.5kg, gutted and scaled
salt and ground black pepper
200ml fish stock
2 lemons, halved

SALAD

1 medium aubergine
12 small new potatoes, halved
200g green beans
4 tablespoons olive oil
coarsely ground black pepper
12 cherry tomatoes, halved
2 tablespoons sultanas
1 teaspoon chopped red chilli
100g mixed salad leaves

PESTO

50g whole unskinned almonds,
20g pecorino cheese, grated
2 garlic cloves, finely chopped
20 fresh basil leaves
6–8 tablespoons olive oil

Baking the whole carp makes things easy, leaving you to concentrate on the salad and pesto. There are some big flavours here, but they work very well in my view. It's also nice to be able to present the whole fish on the table and allow people to help themselves. Just be careful not to overcook the fish, as it will fall apart – remember to slightly undercook and leave the residual heat to do the rest.

1___Preheat the oven to 220°C/Gas 7.

2___Cut the aubergine into 1cm dice and diagonally slice the green beans, then toss with the potatoes in the olive oil and pepper on a baking tray. Spread out and bake for 20 minutes or until the potatoes are cooked through. Remove from the oven and leave to cool.

3___Meanwhile, spread 3 tablespoons of the oil for the fish over the base of a baking dish, add the fish and season well. Add the stock and lemon halves, then the remaining olive oil. Cover with foil and bake for 12–15 minutes until slightly undercooked; do not overcook. Remove from the oven, cover loosely with foil and leave to rest in a warm place for at least 5 minutes.

4___Lightly toast the almonds then put with all the other ingredients for the pesto into a blender with salt and pepper and whizz until fairly smooth. Spoon into a bowl and check the seasoning and consistency.

5___Once the vegetables are cooled, mix gently with the tomatoes, sultanas, chilli and salad leaves and season well.

8___To serve, carefully place the fish on a warm plate, spoon over some of the cooking juices and serve the salad and pesto separately.

Spicy Carp Fritters
with Sweet & Sour Tangerine Dipping Sauce

SERVES 4
Preparation: 10 mins
Cooking: about 15 mins

vegetable oil, for deep-frying
200g self-raising flour, plus
  extra for coating
about 200ml sparkling water
  or lager
250g filleted carp, or 2 carp
  fillets, skinned
salt

DIPPING SAUCE
4 tablespoons soy sauce
1 tablespoon toasted sesame
  oil
1 tablespoon peeled and
  chopped fresh ginger
2 tablespoons dry sherry
2 tablespoons runny honey
2 spring onions, finely
  shredded on a slight angle
finely grated zest of 4 small
  tangerines, clementines or
  satsumas, and juice of 1
4 tablespoons roughly
  chopped fresh coriander

This recipe is a nod to my friend Ken Hom who introduced me to the joys of tangerine as a seasoning and ingredient.

1___Heat vegetable oil for deep-frying in a deep-fat fryer or deep saucepan to 180°C.

2___Meanwhile, for the dipping sauce, put the soy sauce, sesame oil, ginger, sherry and honey into a bowl.

3___Add the spring onions and citrus zest and juice, then the coriander and mix well.

4___Put the flour into a large bowl and then beat in enough sparkling water or lager to make a thickish batter, but do not overwhisk.

5___Cut the carp into long 2cm strips and pat dry with kitchen paper.

6___Toss the carp strips in a little flour, then dip into the batter.

7___Deep-fry in small batches for 2–3 minutes, then remove with a slotted spoon, drain well on kitchen paper and keep hot while you fry the rest.

8___Sprinkle the fritters with a little salt and serve hot with the dipping sauce.

ZANDER

This freshwater fish came to our shores, depending on which piece of information you believe, anywhere from the early 1900s way up to the 1950s. It can grow to a fair size, well over 5kg, and has a full, firm texture with a good flavour that compares well with cod or haddock. Although still caught in canals and rivers in the UK, it's fairly uncommon; they are often caught only to protect the river eco system because, like pike, they are voracious hunters. These days, most zander come from the former states of the Soviet Union and the current Russian Federation, and are perfectly good and highly sustainable. A frozen fillet is relatively easy to purchase and delivers consistently good results even for the sceptics who say river fish are inferior to sea fish. Hungarians love it and eat a lot.

Seared Zander with Egg, Capers & Herbs

SERVES 4
Preparation: 15 mins, plus infusing
Cooking: 10 mins

2 tablespoons olive oil
finely grated zest of 2 large
   unwaxed limes
4 x 175g–200g zander fillets,
   skinned
salt and ground black pepper
225g selection of salad leaves
   or a few baby spinach leaves
   and soft fresh herbs

DRESSING
2 medium hard-boiled eggs,
   finely sieved or chopped
1 tablespoon chopped capers
4 medium gherkins, chopped
2 tablespoons chopped parsley
2 shallots, very finely chopped
6 teaspoons extra virgin olive
   oil
finely grated zest and juice of
   ½ unwaxed lemon

A hearty, pungent herb and egg dressing is perfect with zander fillets – it's almost like a tartare sauce without the mayonnaise. If you can make the dressing and then leave it for an hour or two, all the better. I always cook with a second-pressed olive oil and use extra virgin only for the end dressing in order to preserve its wonderful colour and flavour.

1___Mix the olive oil with the lime zest and leave to infuse for 20 minutes, then strain through a fine sieve. You will have a lovely greenish oil with a fresh lime aroma.

2___For the dressing, put the eggs, capers, gherkins, parsley and shallots into a bowl.

3___Add the extra virgin olive oil and the lemon zest and juice, season well with salt and pepper and leave to infuse for a few minutes.

4___Preheat a griddle pan or frying pan over a high heat.

5___Meanwhile, spoon the lime oil all over the zander fillets and season well with salt and pepper.

6___Add the fish to the very hot pan and cook for 2–3 minutes on each side. Do not overcook.

7___Remove the fish from the pan, then place on a warm plate, cover loosely with foil and leave in a warm place to rest for 5 minutes. The centre of the fish should be warm but slightly undercooked when served.

8___To serve, arrange a few salad leaves in the centre of a large plate, top with the zander and spoon over the dressing.

Grilled Zander with Orange Butter Sauce

SERVES 4
Preparation: 10 mins
Cooking: about 15 mins

4 x 200g (give or take) zander
   fillets, skin on
4 tablespoons olive oil
salt and freshly ground black
   pepper

SAUCE
finely grated zest and juice of
   2 large unwaxed (organic)
   oranges
300ml strong fish stock
2 shallots, finely chopped
a small pinch of dried chilli
   flakes
75g ice-cold unsalted butter,
   diced

Any lightly cooked fish can be paired with citrus butter sauce. The sharpness brings out the flavour of Zander perfectly in my view. This also means that a little sauce can go a long way, so do not drown the fish, use it more like a seasoning.

SAUCE

1___Put the orange juice, fish stock, shallots and chilli into a saucepan and cook over a fairly high heat until reduced by two-thirds. Reserve the orange zest for serving.

2___Whisk in the cold butter until you have a thickened sauce, then season well with salt and pepper.

ZANDER

1___While the sauce is cooking, preheat the grill to its hottest setting.

2___Slash the skin of the fish in a crisscross fashion, then brush with some of the olive oil and season well on both sides.

3___Use the rest of the olive oil to oil a non-stick baking tray, then place the zander on the oiled tray skin side up and grill for about 6–8 minutes, basting occasionally. Do not overcook the fish.

4___Carefully lift the fish onto a warm serving plate.

TO FINISH

1___Stir the orange zest into the sauce to keep its oily freshness and then spoon over the fillets.

2___Serve straight away, with a simple dressed mixed leaf salad and crusty bread.

CRAYFISH

Our native white-clawed crayfish had been happily living here in the UK for centuries and thrived in many of our streams and lakes. Then in the 1970s along came the American Signal crayfish, introduced to these shores as a cool business venture. When the bottom fell out of the market, the blighters were released into our waterways, thus causing a real headache. Like a lot of river dwellers, they are voracious hunters and will stop at pretty much nothing, even eatng their own offspring. They also eat our native fish and have a water-borne virus that kills our fish too. The enviroment agency believes that up to as much as 50 per cent of native stocks of crayfish have disappeared and the onward march of the invaders shows no signs of slowing.

I remember ten years ago watching two Polish lads catching crayfish in a stream, and they were so exited. They had a huge bucket and could not wait to get home and cook them. Despite being a serious pest, you still have to have a licence to trap or fish for them in the UK. My brother's son loves to catch them near Oxford and they grill them on the barbecue – delicious.

Potted Spiced Crayfish with Toasted Sunflower Seed Rye Bread

SERVES 4
Preparation: 20 mins, plus chilling and softening
Cooking: 10 mins

50g unsalted butter, plus another 120g melted
4 large shallots, finely chopped
3 garlic cloves, finely chopped
250g cooked peeled crayfish tails
salt and freshly ground black pepper
2 pinches of chilli powder
a pinch of paprika
finely grated zest and juice 1 large unwaxed lemon
4 tablespoons chopped fresh parsley
120g unsalted butter, melted
8 slices of seed bread, toasted and cut into long triangles

This is a nice way to start a meal, or eat on its own with a chilled glass of white wine. The important thing is to remove the finished dish from the fridge an hour before you serve or the butter will be too cold.

1___Heat the 50g butter gently in a saucepan, add the shallots and garlic and cook for 5 minutes until softened but not coloured.

2___Cut the crayfish tails in half, add to the garlic and shallots and mix well to warm through.

3___Season well with salt and pepper and the chilli powder and paprika, and really mix well.

4___Spoon into a bowl, then add the lemon zest and juice and the parsley and mix well again.

5___Finally, add the melted butter and mix well.

6___Spoon the mixture into a nice deep serving dish, one that's deep enough to submerge the crayfish perfectly. Cover the dish with clingfilm and chill well, preferably overnight.

7___When ready to serve, remove from the fridge at least 1 hour before eating to let the butter soften to room temperature.

8___Serve spooned onto the triangles of toast, or let your guests help themselves.

Easy Crayfish Soup

SERVES 2

Preparation: 20 mins

Cooking: about 20 mins

25g unsalted butter

1 tablespoon olive oil

2 shallots, finely chopped

1 small celery stick, finely
chopped

2 garlic cloves, finely chopped

250g whole crayfish or crayfish
or other fish shells

2 sprigs of fresh tarragon

50ml brandy

50ml white wine

400–450ml fish stock (from a
cube is fine)

about 100ml double cream

a pinch of smoked paprika

juice of ½ lemon

salt and freshly ground black
pepper

2 tablespoons chopped fresh
chives

This soup is so rich in texture and flavour that it's hard to believe it's so easy to make. You could obviously replace the crayfish shells with cracked lobster or crab shells, or try using good-quality whole shrimps, which would be a bit more pricey but still good. It's a great way to use up shells of any description.

1___Melt the butter with the oil in a saucepan, add the shallots, celery and garlic and cook gently for 1–2 minutes until softened but not coloured.

2___Increase the heat, add the crayfish or shells to the pan with the tarragon and cook for another minute or two, stirring.

3___Pour in the brandy and wine and allow to reduce right down.

4___Stir in the stock and bring to the boil, then boil fast for 10–12 minutes to cook and reduce.

5___Transfer to a blender or food-processor and whizz to break up the shells.

6___Strain into a clean saucepan through a very fine sieve, pressing down with the back of a wooden spoon.

7___Stir in the cream and add the paprika and lemon juice. Season to taste and just heat through gently.

8___Ladle into warm bowls and add a tiny sprinkling of the chives to each one.

PIKE

Pike is like Marmite – you either love it or hate it. Why? Well, from a chef's point of view it can be a real pain, as there are so many bones, so it's a fiddly job. From a diner's point of view, a lot of people dislike it because they are conscious of the fact that it's a bottom-dwelling pond fish. The first I can sympathise with, but don't be put off on the second count. It can be a superb fish to eat, firm with a great flavour. I once had steamed fillet of pike with sorrel sauce in the Loire Valley and it was fantastic, being marred only by my friend getting a bone stuck in her throat! That aside, it's also great value for money. A lot of trout fisheries here in the UK pay anglers to catch pike in the close season, as they are prolific hunters. The best time of the year to enjoy them is during the winter, as the flesh is particularly good at that time of year. The traditional way to cook pike is quenelles – basically, pike flesh puréed with egg white and cream. It's never been a favourite of mine, so here, instead, I have brought the humble pike right up to date with a raita.

Pan-fried Pike Fillet with Carrot Raita

SERVES 4
Preparation: 20 mins
Cooking: about 5 mins, plus resting

2–3 tablespoons olive oil
4 x 150g fillet steaks of pike, skinned
salt and freshly ground black pepper

RAITA

5 medium carrots, peeled and finely grated
85g raisins
a pinch of chilli powder
1 tablespoon caster sugar
finely grated zest and juice of 2 large unwaxed limes
150–200g thick natural yogurt
salt

RAITA

1___Put the grated carrots, raisins, chilli powder and sugar into a bowl and mix well.
2___In a separate bowl, add the lime zest and juice to the yogurt, season with salt and mix well.
3___Spoon the yogurt mixture onto the grated carrot mixture and really mix well.

PIKE

1___Heat the olive oil in a non-stick frying pan over a medium heat.
2___Pat the fish dry with kitchen paper and sprinkle with a little salt and pepper, then add to the hot oil and cook for 2–3 minutes.
3___Turn the fish over and cook for a further 2 minutes; do not overcook.
4___Remove from the heat, loosely cover with foil and leave to rest in a warm place for 5 minutes.

TO SERVE

Serve the pike fillets with warm basmati rice and peas, along with the cooling raita.

5   BASICS

Basic Game Stock

MAKES ABOUT 1 LITRE
Preparation: 15 mins
Cooking: 1 hour 45 mins

1 tablespoon any oil, or fat
  from the pheasant carcasses
8 pheasant carcasses, or those
  of other small game – see
  right, chopped into chunks
2 tablespoons red wine vinegar
250ml medium white wine
1 tablespoon tomato purée
1 tablespoon sugar
2 litres cold water, well-
  flavoured chicken stock or 2
  x 10g good-quality chicken
  stock cubes dissolved in 2
  litres hot water
4 carrots, peeled and chopped
3 onions, chopped
1 large leek, split and washed
  well
6 celery sticks, chopped
1 whole head of garlic, sliced
  horizontally in half
3 sprigs of fresh thyme
3 bay leaves
1 teaspoon black peppercorns
1 teaspoon crushed juniper
  berries

Having a good stock base will help the taste and flavour of your dishes immeasurably. You can now buy stock cubes, powders, pouches and even jellied stock, and I think the best approach is to enhance a solid homemade stock base with a little of the shop-bought variety so that you end up with a full-flavoured and full-bodied stock. To me it's all about body and depth, and the more you can help that along the better. This recipe calls for small carcasses such as pheasant, partridge, wild duck and small rabbits or hares, but if you want to use venison, wild boar, large geese and so on, I would advise cooking the stock for slightly longer, say 2 hours 30 minutes, as the bones are larger.

The essential thing to remember is that the longer a cooked and strained stock is returned to the hob to cook down or reduce, the stronger its flavour will be. A simply strained, unreduced stock is ideal for stews and braises, as you are going to intensify the flavours further with added meats, seasonings and vegetables, whereas a stock reduced by simmering and skimming to about half its original volume is great for light sauces, adding to stir-fries and for broth and soup making. Stock fully reduced to 15–20 per cent of its original volume is for when you want to pack a punch with very little sauce. In this instance, you can add a dash of alcohol, a fruit liqueur or just a little ice-cold butter to bring out the shine and depth of a sauce. This is known in the business as a *glace*.

1___Heat the oil or render the fat in a large saucepan. Add the chunks of carcass and brown well on all sides. This will add colour and flavour to the stock.

2___Add the vinegar, white wine, tomato purée and sugar, bring to the boil and cook until the liquid has almost completely evaporated. Stir well, scraping up any of the bits stuck to the base of the pan.

3___Pour over the water or stock, add all the vegetables and garlic and bring to the boil, then reduce to a simmer and cook for 10 minutes.

4___Skim well and add the herbs, peppercorns and juniper. Simmer for a further 1 hour 20 minutes.

5___Strain the stock and use accordingly.

Game Pie

SERVES 6–8
Preparation: 30–40 mins,
plus marinating and chilling
Cooking: about 2 hours

No game book is complete with a game pie recipe, so here is mine. It's not quick, but it is well worth the time spent. Do not rush it. If you were to use a little less meat, you could add more jellied stock.

FILLING

750g fatty pork, finely chopped
1kg mixed game meat, thighs
   and breasts, not drumsticks,
   cut into 3cm cubes
2 sprigs of fresh rosemary
1 teaspoon dried thyme
1 teaspoon each ground
   cinnamon and ground cloves
½ teaspoon each ground mace,
   nutmeg and allspice
100ml Madeira or dry sherry
2 tablespoons olive oil
2 tablespoons red wine vinegar
salt and black pepper
2 tablespoons finely chopped
   fresh parsley

PASTRY

200ml water
175g lard
salt
500g plain flour
2 tablespoons icing sugar
a pinch of black pepper

TO FINISH

3 tablespoons powdered
   gelatine
225ml strong chicken stock or
   game stock (see page 214)
1 medium egg, beaten

FILLING

1___Put all the ingredients for the filling, apart from the parsley, into a glass or metallic bowl and mix together well.
2___Cover the bowl with clingfilm and leave to marinate in the fridge overnight.

PASTRY

1___The next day, put the water, lard and a couple pinches of salt into a saucepan and bring to the boil.
2___Put the flour, icing sugar, a pinch of salt and the pepper into the bowl of an electric mixer fitted with a dough hook and mix together on a slow speed for 3–4 minutes.
3___Add the boiling liquid and mix until well incorporated, then cover the bowl with clingfilm and leave to cool completely.

PIE

1___Preheat the oven to 190°C/Gas 5.
2___Take three-quarters of the pastry and roll out on a floured work surface until large enough to line a 24cm round, 5.5cm deep, baking tin with a generous overlap – don't make it too thick. Trim off the excess pastry, leaving 2–3cm.
3___Put the meat mixture into the pastry case and top with the parsley, leaving the filling sitting nicely proud of the top of the tin.
4___Brush the top edge of the pastry case with beaten egg.
5___Roll out the remaining quarter of the pastry and lay on top of the pie, then seal well and neaten the edge.
6___Brush the pastry lid well with beaten egg, then cut out a small hole, about 1cm round, in the middle of the pie.
7___Bake for 35 minutes, then reduce the heat to 160°C/Gas 3 and bake for a further 1 hour 30 minutes. Remove the pie from the oven leave to cool slightly.

TO FINISH

1___Heat the gelatine with the stock in a small saucepan until thoroughly dissolved.
2___Using a small jug, carefully pour the hot stock through the hole in the lid into the pie until it overflows. Tap the tin gently and refill if necessary.
3___Carefully transfer the pie to the fridge and chill overnight.
4___Serve cut into big wedges and serve with piccalilli, pickle or pickled red cabbage.

Game Pasta Braise

SERVES 4
Preparation: 20 mins, plus soaking (optional)
Cooking: about 50 mins, plus cooling

3 tablespoons olive oil
2 onions, finely chopped
2 garlic cloves, chopped
2 teaspoons dried oregano
500g cooked or raw game meat, cut into 2cm pieces
1 small glass red wine (optional)
400–500ml game stock (see page 214) or game gravy (see page 217)
100g dried green lentils, soaked in cold water overnight and drained (or canned will do if drained, rinsed well and drained again)
about 200g cooked pasta – I like to use spaghetti, roughly chopped
salt and freshly ground black pepper

Yes, I know it sounds odd, but stay with me on this. I once had a dish in northern Italy that was part stew, part stir-fry and part bake and it tasted really delicious. It used goose and had an incredibly deep flavour and colour. It seemed to me to be a sort of 'use up' peasant dish and reminded me of the superb Piedmontaise dish that stews veal tendons with cockscombs and sweetbreads, and that takes days to make. I use any cooked game meat; raw game will also work here.

1___Preheat the oven to 220°C/Gas 7.

2___Heat the oil in an ovenproof sauté pan with a lid. Add the onions, garlic and oregano and cook over a high heat for 3 minutes.

3___Add the game meat and red wine (if using) and cook until almost all the wine has evaporated.

4___Add the stock or gravy, lentils and pasta and stir well. Check the seasoning and adjust if necessary and then bring to the boil.

5___Put the lid on, transfer the pan to the oven and cook for 20 minutes. Then remove the lid and cook for a further 20–25 minutes until the sauce reduces and the stew thickens – don't go mad.

6___Remove from the oven and leave to cool for 15 minutes. Serve just as it is!

Game Gravy

SERVES 6-8
Preparation: 10 mins
Cooking: about 1 hour, plus standing

500–750g game bones, roughly chopped, the smaller the better

2 carrots, peeled and finely chopped

1 onion, finely chopped

2 celery sticks, finely chopped

1 small leek, split, washed well and finely chopped

1 large glass wine – I normally use white wine for birds and rabbits; red wine for geese, large venison (not Muntjac) and hares.

2–3 tablespoons plain flour

800ml hot chicken stock or water and 2 x 10g good-quality chicken stock cubes, crumbled

salt and freshly ground black pepper

1 tablespoon redcurrant or apple jelly

No one makes gravy any more – it's a 'jus' or, even more annoying, an 'essence of'. I was always taught that gravy comes in two guises: thin, meaning meat juices from the roast or stock from a boiled silverside or ham, and thickened, using a little flour or other starch. Now, of course, you can buy gravy granules, which are basically powdered stock, flavourings and starch granules, but it's very easy to make your own gravy. I tend to make a lot at the weekend if we are having a roast and then use it all week to brighten up our weekly meals. This recipe is for small game bones such as those from rabbit or small game birds, but if you use big venison or large geese bones, the simmering time should be longer, say an hour to get the best flavour. A good tip here is to chop the vegetables as finely as possible so that they not only cook more quickly but all their flavour and nutrients are released efficiently. This freezes perfectly.

1___Preheat the oven to 220°C/Gas 7.

2___Put the bones and vegetables together into a roasting tray and roast for 15 minutes until well coloured.

3___Transfer the tray to the hob and cook until really well browned.

4___Remove from the heat and push all the bones and veg to one end of the tray, then put a wooden spoon under that end so that the fat runs to the other end of the tray. Leave for 10 minutes, then spoon off the fat and discard.

5___Place the tray back on the hob, then add the wine and simmer, scraping up all the lovely caught pieces from the base of the tray.

6___Tip into a saucepan and boil until the wine has almost all evaporated.

7___Add the flour, coating the bones well, then stir in the hot stock or water and stock cubes and bring to the boil.

8___Simmer gently for 25 minutes, taking care as the gravy will reduce and may burn slightly, so stir occasionally. Once cooked and nicely thickened, taste and season if necessary, then add the redcurrant or apple jelly and stir to dissolve it in the gravy.

9___Strain through a fine sieve and re-boil to use when needed. This will freeze perfectly.

Savoy Cabbage & Onions

SERVES 4
Preparation time 5 minutes
Cooking time about 20 minutes

75g unsalted butter

2 tablespoons extra virgin olive oil

1 small onion, very thinly sliced

2 sprigs of fresh rosemary

1 small Savoy cabbage, very finely shredded

4 tablespoons vegetable stock or water

salt and freshly ground black pepper

Any cabbage works well with game – its earthy, sweet flavour is a perfect foil for game meats. The secret here is to cook the cabbage in the water or stock (a small pinch of good-quality vegetable stock cube is okay here) to evaporate it off, at the same time as softening the vegetable and glazing it nicely with butter.

1 Heat the butter and oil in a large saucepan until just bubbling.

2 Add the onion and rosemary, season well with salt and pepper and stir over a medium heat for about 10–15 minutes until the onion has softened.

3 Add the cabbage and stir-fry over a high heat for 2 minutes until it softens slightly.

4 Add the vegetable stock or water, season well with salt and pepper and cook over a high heat until the liquid evaporates and the butter coats the cabbage well.

Sweet Pickled Quinces

MAKES ONE 750ML JAR
Preparation: 10 mins, plus cooling
Cooking: 45 mins–1 hour 15 mins

2 large ripe quinces with a wonderful aroma (700g total weight)

500g granulated sugar

500ml cold water

juice of 2 large limes

1 Put the quinces into a stainless steel saucepan along with the sugar, water and lime juice. The quinces must be covered with the liquid.

2 Bring to the boil, then cover with a lid and simmer very gently until the fruit is soft. This can take as little as 45 minutes or as long as 1 hour 15 minutes, depending on the size, variety and ripeness of the fruits. To test, use a skewer and pierce the fruit – there will be a little resistance due to the core of the fruit, and this will not soften by cooking, but the rest of the fruit should be soft and succulent.

3 Remove the pan from the stove and leave to cool with the lid on.

4 Transfer the quinces to a glass or ceramic bowl and pour over the syrup to cover. Cover the bowl with clingfilm and chill until needed. To store – the fruit will keep perfectly in the syrup for up to 1 month in the fridge – transfer to a sterilised 750ml Kilner jar and seal.

Glossary

AIR-DRIED
A generic term describing a product that has been cured and undergone a lengthy maturation period. How long this maturation takes depends on the thickness of the product, so the thinner it is the quicker it will be.

BREAD RUSK
A form of breadcrumb commonly used to help bind and provide texture to a sausage. It will also soak up twice its weight in water.

BRINE
A solution of water and curing salt used primarily for curing bacon and ham.

CURING SALT
Salt that has been blended with a curing agent. In salami production, for example, it often contains 0.6% sodium nitrite.

DEADWEIGHT
The term used to describe the carcass weight of any animal that has been slaughtered.

DEXTROSE
Commercial glucose, commonly used in the production of salamis.

FAT CONTENT
The amount of fat required to make a product. Within the trade, cuts of meat are bought according to how much visual lean meat (%vl) is needed.

FEE (EMULSIFYING AGENT)
Typically, e471, the mono and diglyceride fatty acid commonly used as an emulsifier and stabiliser in pâté-like products.

HOT SMOKED
A product that is cooked in a smoke-filled environment, typically at temperatures of between 75 and 85°C. Any kind of hardwood can be used for this process.

LACTIC ACID
One of the by-products of fermentation in a salami. Lactobacillus and pediococcus bacteria metabolise (feed on) the sugar content and produce lactic acid.

NATURAL CASINGS
The small intestine of pigs, sheep or cattle, which, cleaned and brined (salted), is used to make a whole host of products from chipolatas to salami.

PAVE
Hog casing that has been dried and formed into sheets so it can be wrapped around products such as coppa and lomo.

PH METER/PH
A device that accurately measures acidic and alkaline levels. A must-have for food safety if you are producing salami or any other fermented product.

POTASSIUM NITRATE
More commonly known as saltpetre, this is used as a curing agent in curing salt. Its use is strictly regulated and it is always best to source from reputable suppliers who will certify how much has been used.

REDDENING
The term commonly used to describe the fermentation process in salamis. They start off a dismal grey colour and after the starter cultures have worked their magic they turn a lovely red colour.

RELATIVE HUMIDITY
The ratio of partial pressure of water vapour in an air–water mixture to the saturated vapour pressure of water at a certain temperature. It's particularly relevant in the production of salamis and air-dried products.

SALTPETRE
See Potassium nitrate.

SODIUM ASCORBATE
The salt of ascorbic acid. Mostly used as a curing accelerator and anti-oxidant. It is typically used in all products that are made with curing salt.

SODIUM NITRITE
Used as a curing agent in curing salt, for example in the production of salamis.

SOUS VIDE
The French term for 'under vacuum', it is a method of cooking whereby food is sealed in airtight bags and cooked in water at lower temperatures and for longer periods of time than in conventional cooking.

STARTER CULTURE
Bacteria such as lactobacillus that feed on sugars and produce lactic acid. Used in the fermentation process, it is responsible for giving salami its distinctive flavour and for lowering the pH value of the product.

TEMPERED
Frozen meat that has been placed in a fridge and allowed to soften.

VACUUM COOKING
See Sous vide.

Stockists

MEAT & INGREDIENTS

The Best Butchers
Simon Boddy's butchery.
www.thebestbutchers.co.uk
Unit 5, Lower Rectory Farm,
Great Brickhill, Milton Keynes.
01908 375275

Continental Meat Technology
Seasonings, functional
ingredients, herbs and spices for
sausages, hams, bacon, cooked
and cured meats, including
the specialist flavourings
mentioned in this book.
*www. continental
meattechnology.co.uk*
01908 584489

Weschenfelder
Sausage making supplies,
from casings and seasonings
to mincers, knives and
smoking machines.
www.weschenfelder.co.uk

SMOKING & CURING EQUIPMENT

Arden Smoker Supplies
www.foodsmoker.co.uk

Bradley Smoker
www.bradleysmoker.co.uk

Hot Smoked
www.hotsmoked.co.uk

PH Meters and Food Thermometers
www.digital-meters.com
www.thermometer.co.uk

AUSTRALIA

www.butcherathome.com.au

Department of Agriculture,
Fisheries and Forestry (DAFF)
www.daff.gov.au

NEW ZEALAND

www.bradleysmoker.co.nz
www.thecasingboutique.co.nz
www.kitchenshop.co.nz

Ministry for Primary
Industries (MPI)
www.mpi.govt.nz

SOUTH AFRICA

www.thebutcherweb.co.za
www.crownnational.co.za

Department for Agriculture,
Forestry and Fisheries
www.nda.agric.za

Index

For Peter Applewhite – Phil
For Tina & Jack – Simon

Acknowledgements

Putting a book together like this takes an immense amount of time and effort. So my thanks to all of you however large or small your contribution. Kyle, many thanks again for still having faith in what we do. Simon, another brilliant piece of work; you have probably forgotten more than I know, you never fail to come up with some fabulous recipes, plus you make me smile! Beautiful, stunning photography from Pete Cassidy. Many thanks to Judith Hannam, for not hassling me, even though she supports a dodgy football club.

John Rush and Luigi Bonomi, for all the guidance and help. Bruce and Willie Laughton, Parto, Big Phil Scotney and all the lads at the Rufford. Trevor Smith, Paul Vidic, Simon Freeman and Peter Gott. Mike Bryant, best fisherman I've ever met and who always takes the piss when I lose a fish.

Grade Design (Peter Dawson, Paul Palmer-Edwards and Namkwan Cho), copy-editor, Jo Richardson, editorial assistant, Claire Rogers, and Gemma John and Nic Jones in production.

Finally love and thanks to my wife Fern, you're my best mate!!!

Phil Vickery

As a passionate follower of country sports, especially salmon fishing and game shooting, I can't thank Phil enough for asking me to help with this book.

The photography is amazing again, thanks to Pete Cassidy (who had a great time in Scotland). Many thanks, too, to Bedford Estates at Woburn, and to Dan from the Deer Department for a great day photographing. And to Judith and all her team at Kyle Books (including Grade Design) for making this a very special book. Just amazing...

Simon Boddy

First published in Great Britain in 2014 by
Kyle Books, an imprint of Kyle Cathie Ltd
192–198 Vauxhall Bridge Road
London SW1V 1DX
general.enquiries@kylebooks.com
www.kylebooks.com

10 9 8 7 6 5 4 3 2 1

ISBN 978 0 85783 103 3

Editor: Judith Hannam
Editorial Assisant: Claire Rogers
Copy Editor: Jo Richardson
Designer: Grade Design
Photographer: Peter Cassidy
Food Stylist: Mima Sinclair
Prop Stylist: Iris Bromet
Production: Nic Jones and Gemma John

A Cataloguing in Publication record for this title is available from the British Library.

Colour reproduction by ALTA London
Printed and bound in Slovenia by DZS Grafik d.o.o

Important Note The information and advice contained in this book are intended as a general guide to curing and smoking and is based on the authors' own experimentation, experience and research. Neither the authors nor the publishers can be held responsible for the consequences of the application or misapplication of any of the information or ideas presented in this book.